PART-TIME

TIME

PROGRAMMER

An Easy & Proven Way to Teach Yourself to Code.

JON DOUGLAS

To my beautiful wife Stevie, daughter Audrey, and son

Jack. I love you all to the moon and back.

Table of Contents

CHAPTER ONE

Introduction

* * *

In other words, why you should even care.

* * *

👋 Welcome

Hey friends, welcome to the part-time programmer. The fact that you are reading or watching the course means you took the first step towards making programming a skill that you can leverage in your life. But first, a little about me.

🐱 My Story

I started learning how to program in my final years of high school by building websites. It wasn't until college where I would write my first actual program. After college, I started my journey into the workforce only to realize that I wasn't prepared at all. I felt like I should know enough to at least land a job, but I could barely write code & would be stumped in technical interviews.

Today however, I've been working at Microsoft for over 5 years while building some of the coolest developer tools on the market. Anything is possible.

😐 The Secret to Becoming a Software Engineer

Over the past 3 years, I've learned a lot about what it takes to help aspiring developers land software jobs. And you know what? There's no secret. It's mostly just a matter of:

1. Choosing the right skills to learn.
2. Rapidly learning new skills.
3. Repeating this for 6-12 months.

That's all it takes. I can guarantee that if you follow this simple, 3-part formula, your life will change in ways you can't imagine. You'll learn incredibly useful skills you can take anywhere, land one of the most respected jobs in tech, and you'll even make a career out of it.

But sadly, as with all things, getting started and maintaining passion & perseverance is easier said than done.

🎯 The Challenges

6-12 months is a long time. You won't see much growth, or much progress in the early stages. You'll have to get over the fear of judgement from friends, family, and strangers on the internet. You'll have to figure out what you're going to learn, and why anyone would care if your skills are worthy of a job.

You'll need to learn about programming, frameworks, technology stacks, data structures & algorithms, software engineering, and much more. You'll worry that you're not learning the right things. You'll be constantly thinking about whether you are prepared enough for a whiteboard interview. You'll end up negotiating with companies over compensation because you have no idea how much you're actually worth.

And you'll have to do all this (and a lot more) while balancing your job, education, relationships, and health. All while doing your best to enjoy the journey and avoid burnout.

This is hard. It takes a lot of work. But it's also really fun, and if you can make it work, it's genuinely life-changing.

If there's one real "secret" that I could give to you, it is that you must build a SYSTEM around your software developer journey, so you can efficiently learn the tech that is being used by startups, big tech, and unicorns alike without it taking up large amounts of your own time.

Instead of thinking of your developer journey as a personal project, you want to think about it like a SYSTEM. A system that takes inputs in the form of ideas & projects, and outputs valuable experiences that companies will love and hire you on the spot.

I've built such a system for my software career and business, and I can help you build yours.

The Part-Time Programmer

I'll teach you everything I know about how to build and grow your software engineering career into a sustainable, streamlined system that (a) outputs valuable skills, (b) appeals to tech employers, and (c) generates a healthy balance for you, without you having to quit your job.

* * *

It's based on my personal system I've developed to grow my career from being an entry level software engineer to a senior program manager at Microsoft in less than 5 years.

By the end of this book

- You'll have started your developer journey and published 4 blogs.
- You'll have the next 3-6 months of skills to learn planned out.
- You'll be comfortable taking on new languages & technologies.
- You'll have a system that ensures you'll never run out of skills to learn, projects to build, or opportunities to pursue.
- You'll have my method for structuring your blogs in a way that appeals to a public audience and to search algorithms.
- You'll learn how to build in the public and repurpose your code to help others.
- You'll understand how to perfect your developer portfolio and give employers something nice to look at.
- You'll know the value of rapid skill acquisition and you'll be able to pickup anything new quickly.
- You'll learn about the important principles, strategies, and tools to maximize your productivity as a programmer, to help you maintain consistency without programming taking over your life.

Who's the book for?

The book is aimed at people who (like me) want to treat programming as a skill first-and-foremost. Yes, programming is a great skill for building with others, automating boring tasks, and having an impact in business. But if it wasn't one of the most viable business assets in my eyes, I wouldn't be spending so much time on creating this book.

Rockstar Beginners

- You recognize programming as an incredible opportunity to build a relevant skill in a tech dominated world.
- You haven't quite taken the plunge into programming, but you know it's something you want to do. Maybe you've even been held back by the fear of being judged, fighting off perfectionism, or not knowing what you should learn.

- You're willing to take this book seriously from day 1, and want to invest time and money to set yourself up for success with programming.
- In a month - You'll have launched your blog with 4+ published blogs and thoughts about your next 3-6 months of learning.

Intermediate Developers
- Congratulations! You likely already got a degree, gone through a bootcamp, or landed a programming job.
- But you've realized that staying relevant in tech is a vicious cycle and your daily job is learning new skills fast.
- You'd love to treat programming as more of a business with you as the CEO and aim towards climbing the career ladder or building your own company/product. But maybe the idea feels intimidating and you wouldn't know where to start anyway.
- In a month - You'll have new ideas for the relevant skills in the industry today, the basics of validating the feasibility of side projects generating real passive income, and know how to take the first steps. You may even pick up some useful tips along the way.

Entrepreneurs & Freelancers
- You see programming as the next skill you need to learn to engage with your target audience and generate leads, awareness, or even automate tasks for your business. You've got a ton of experimental learning from growing your business already that you'd love to develop into a software product that makes money for you while you sleep.
- But learning to program has always been pushed to the bottom of your endless to-do list. It falls into the important but not urgent category so it never gets done or you outsource the job and get less than ideal results making you work harder than you have to.
- In a month - You'll have an understanding of how to make programming work for you, and a good idea of what it takes to build a wealth-generating software product from the ground up that makes you money while you sleep.

* * *

📚 What's In The Book?

👋 **Introduction** - Why learning how to program is the best investment you can make in 2021. You'll learn about the demand of software developers, why self-taught is important for your career, and embracing life-long learning to accelerate your journey.

💭 **Mindset** - How to get into the programmer's mindset by unlearning everything you know today. I'll help you get comfortable with the fact that anyone can learn to program with the right mindset. You'll learn about thinking slow & how you can be productive with your procrastination.

🏰 **System** - How to build a system of learning effectively & efficiently. You'll use agile methods to plan & execute on perfecting your developer skills. You'll learn about managing your energy, flow, and willpower without burning out.

🧭 **Roadmap** - How to create your own developer journey with a plethora of online resources. No developer's journey is the same, and you'll be empowered when building your own. You'll learn about some of the best resources out there on the internet while also deconstructing developer jobs to learn the right skills.

🔄 **Habits** - How to not rely on motivation and get into habits that will take you closer everyday to your goals. You'll learn how to debug you bad habits & replace them with good ones, and how to break down intimidating tasks into manageable chunks.

📚 **Skills** - How to rapidly acquire new skills using scientifically-proven techniques that will help you learn faster, retain more, and match your learning style to make learning fun. You'll avoid the common time wasters & be able to take any new skill head-on.

👤 **Job** - How to write a kick-ass resume & developer portfolio that will have employers hiring you on the spot. You'll learn how to prepare for a job by writing cover letters that stand out & how to make the most of an interview that will make you stand out.

Building - How to learn faster by building personal projects, contributing to open source, and building in public all while showing off your amazing developer skills.

Career - How to accelerate your career by finding a mentor, choosing a career path, moving jobs when needed, and getting regular raises.

Validate - How to validate any idea to save you time before you write a single line of code. You'll learn how to get to a minimal viable product & talk to your users to make sure you're building the right thing.

○ **Workflows** - How to maximize your daily workflows by introducing deep & shallow work sessions, getting into regular flow state, and optimizing the time you're actually working.

Homework Assignments
The homework assignments are an important part of the book. Reading this book will only get you so far. It would be like signing up for a class, reading the syllabus, and not doing any of the work. It might be interesting, but it will not get you any results.

You can't break into the tech industry without consistently putting in work every week. In general, you need to work at least once a week for the odds to be in your favor.

Each week, I'll give you an assignment which will involve coding, building, writing, and getting out of your comfort zone. When you're done, you'll share your work with the world to give you feedback.

Let's get started
Alright, you now know what this course is all about. Now let's talk about why learning to program is a good idea & how you can make the most out of your journey of teaching yourself to code.

* * *

Why Learn Programming

A computer can do anything you can tell it to do. Let that sink in for a second. Anything. You just have to learn the skills to explain all the steps a computer needs to know.

Technology Is The Future

The world is dominated by technology. The phone you use to scroll through addictive TikToks, the computer that fails to secure your pre-order of the PS5 on launch day, the TV you use to watch three seasons of Cobra Kai on a single Saturday night to name a few.

Software is the future. Being in the software industry from the last 10 years has only proven to me that software is taking over the world.

Why Programming Is Cool

Want to know the cool part about programming? When you know how to program, you are basically guaranteed a job. Okay job security doesn't convince ya yet huh? What about the fact that you don't even need a college degree to get a job programming? Do I have your attention yet? Oh I don't? Okay let's try this one...

How about being able to work at home where pants are completely optional & video game breaks are encouraged? Yeah, that's what I thought...you're getting warmer to the idea. But let's go deeper.
Picture this, you can create anything you want. Remember the whole computers can do anything we tell them to do? Well you get to set the limits to what your app or program can do.

Oh, I forgot to mention one of the coolest parts about this whole learning to program thing. You get paid the big bucks. In fact, most software jobs are approaching the 100k mark for even entry level. Talk about a solid deal. But let's not stop there. Once you start to get competent at programming and understanding what software can do, you will understand new tech much faster. Pretty Cool!

Programming Can Be Hard & Rewarding

Programming can be hard however, and each day gives you the opportunity to solve problems both creatively & elegantly with your technical skills. Imagine your job as a professional problem solver, doesn't that sound awesome?

And if you don't want to solve a company's problems, you can always solve your own problems, share them with the world through open source or even sell your apps on the app stores for others to buy. The opportunities are really endless.

Knowing how to code has so many benefits that if you aren't sitting at the edge of your seat ready to get started, then you may need more coffee, because I'm energized just thinking about the next lesson.

😕 Your Reason To Code

Everyone has their own unique reason to learn how to program. What's yours?

It could be finding a rewarding career where everyday is exciting & new. It could be building a skillset to build an app to help share your passion on indie IPAs that nobody has heard of. It could even be chasing the Benjamins so you can retire early & invest in whatever you want. There should be no judgement in what your unique reasons to code are. These are all valid reasons & will help fuel you with motivation through this book.

😌 Embrace Your Reason

Whatever your reason to code is, you should embrace it. Banking investors embrace the rat-race of pursuing cold hard cash. Doctors embrace their Hippocratic oath when practicing medicine. And you can embrace your reason of why you're learning to code.

For me personally, I embrace the fact that I get to work on cool stuff every single day. Everyday is a new challenge & it makes a career rewarding & interesting. The many benefits such as flexible work, great salaries, and stock options can be just as rewarding & interesting.

😟 Regret Minimization Framework

Making a decision to learn how to code is a big leap that not many take. Consider it in the sense of minimizing your future regrets. If you do not decide to actually learn to code in the next year, and the year after that until you realize you're old and gray, would you have wished you learned how to code while you could? In other words, ask yourself the question of "In X years, will I regret not doing this?". If your answer is yes, you should read on. If the answer is no, then you probably should read another book.

Future-proofing Your Skillset

You may see plenty of opinions about whether or not you should learn to code. Think of it in another way. If you didn't learn to code over the next 10 years, what type of skills do you think would be in demand in 2030? Coding isn't just about being able to give a computer instructions, it's an exercise of problem solving. Learning how to code today gives you a new literacy in a skill that will likely be fundamental in most disciplines.

Paid to learn

Many employers simply cannot catch up with how fast technology moves. The result of this you may ask? Companies willing to pay you to learn on the job. In fact, many companies will send you to conferences multiple times a year just to help expand your knowledge. Every company I've ever been apart of would pay for my pursuits of learning. If that was a $50 textbook on C++ or $500 subscription to a learning platform, companies actually save money by paying the low cost upfront. You'll get more time to teach yourself the most in-demand skills, but the caveat here is that you will continuously have to learn the technical & soft skills to be successful.

Compensated Well

The average base salary for a programmer has increased in the last decade alone. When I got started, 70k was an outstanding salary in a medium-sized city (Salt Lake City for reference). Now that salary has increased well into the six-digits range. If you happen to live in a tech hub, you can expect your salary to be well above this number even to the point where companies will try to incentivize you with other things like paid time off, fitness benefits, stock, and on-hire bonuses.

Stock

One of the best benefits of working for a tech company is being rewarded with stock options or reserved stock. This incentives you to work for the company for a period of time, but it also helps you gauge whether or not the company is successful year after year. Much of your stock will grow with you throughout your career. Having stock early at a company can compound to make you a multi-millionaire at an earlier age than retirement.

Flexible Work

For most programming jobs, your job can be done anywhere in the world where there is an internet connection available. You can work from the comfort of your apartment or home & even your preference of working hours in many cases. I've been lucky enough to work my whole career remotely (10 years to date), and I wouldn't change it for the world. It's allowed me to travel, spend more time with my family, and have the freedom of deciding how I want to work. I've even known people who travel as digital nomads where they will go to exotic places to work from for weeks if not months.

Benefits

There's so many more benefits that may give you reasons to learn to program. Although I could go into details about what each one might be, let's just go through an exhaustive list. How about tuition reimbursement? Free snacks & beverages in the office? Video games in the common rooms? How about fun things to do in-between meetings like foosball, ping pong, or a plethora of board games? Love coffee? They probably have a machine worth more than your first paycheck. If you work on a campus, you might even have access to many sports & activities going on like you would at a college. Many of these benefits are a bit flashy, but they are benefits themselves. For those of you who don't mind being flashy here and there, these are for you.

Demand Of Software Developers

There is a high demand for developer talent & sadly a lack of software developers in the world. The most successful companies & entrepreneurs understand that digital transformation is the path to be successful in the 21st century.

Jobs at risk

Many manual jobs are being automated. Accountants are competing with TurboTax. Truck Drivers are fighting against self-driving vehicles.

Factory workers are head-to-head with robotic supply chain automation. The point is, knowledge jobs tend to be in high demand as they are the ones whose very job is making computers do the one thing they are really good at...following instructions.

Digital Jobs in 2025

By 2025, there will be a capacity for over 150 million digital jobs ranging from cyber security (6 million), data science (20 million), cloud engineering (23 million), and software development (100 million).

The problem however is that there is only about 21 million developers in the world today with an actual capacity of 41 million. That's over 20 million software development jobs being unfulfilled today & companies actually lose out on money every year these positions aren't filled.

Guaranteed a Job

There will be over 100 million potential software jobs over the next 5 years. This means that simply having enough knowledge as a software engineer can guarantee you a job. I can speak personally on this behalf. I've never not had a job in this industry & always have different recruiters & startup founders trying to incentivize me to move. Your skills are heavily in demand, and knowing that will give you the upper hand when it comes time to find a job.

Exploring Your Options

You'll have many options for what you want to do in this industry. Whether you like to build user-facing applications or never want a user to know you wrote the code type options. There's so many options as to what you can do that we'll cover here, but do know that new options appear everyday and you should follow what interests you most.

Front-End Developer

A front-end developer works on the front-end of an application. The front-end is anything a user may interact with on their device. You can think of any experience you have on a website or app to be done by a team of front-end developers.

* * *

Back-end Developer

A back-end developer works on the back-end of an application. The back-end is anything the front-end or internal systems may need to interact with. These are usually APIs and services created by a team of back-end developers to provide data through. You can think of the data or information that populates the front-end to be done by a team of back-end developers.

Full Stack Developer

A full-stack developer works on both the front-end and back-end of an application. They combine the user interactions & APIs for a complete user experience. A developer who uses the full stack of their choosing is typically considered a full stack developer.

Mobile Developer

A mobile developer works on creating the front-end of a mobile platform such as Android or iOS. They are usually responsible for the user-interactions & consumption of APIs to create a complete mobile experience for their users.

Game Developer

A game developer works primarily on the programming aspects of a video game. They work closely with designers, artists, and testers to deliver an entertaining game to their audiences.

Data Scientist

A data scientist will find, clean, and organize data for companies. They analyze large amounts of complex raw information and help find patterns that will benefit an organization to make business decisions.

Database Administrator

A database administrator works on storing and organization of data. They are also responsible for the security, availability, and backup processes for the data they administer.

DevOps Engineer

A DevOps engineer works on creating & managing software releases.

They create devops workflows to ensure software development, testing, and other operations work efficiently.

And Many More

There are many jobs in the software industry that don't quite fit the categories above. Some jobs may even be a hybrid or a "build your own job" type of deal. The beauty of the tech industry is that if you have the skills, you can make your own job & do what you love.

Why Become Self-Taught

Over 70% of people with professional programming backgrounds are self-taught in some capacity. In the fast-paced world of tech, it's becoming even more normalized that people are completely self-taught with no formal education.

Retain More

The biggest benefit of self-taught is the ability to retain more information. Why do you retain more information if you're self-taught? It's mostly because you are following your curiosity. This is a famous method known as "Montessori education" which emphasizes independence and individual choice. This is done by going into large blocks of uninterrupted time & following your natural curiosity.

Self-Paced

Because you're teaching yourself, you can go at a pace that makes sense for you. Some paces of learning might be a bit slow or fast for you. While you're teaching yourself how to program, you're the one who gets to set the pace. If you feel like you master a subject in an afternoon, you follow your intuition to move on to the next thing. You don't have to wait for the rest of the class or feel like you're slowing it down. Rather it's all at your own pace.

Learning Style Preference

There are many different learning style preferences. One famous acronym for learning styles is **VAK:**

- Visual - Learners who learn through written language, reading, and watching lectures.

- Auditory - Learners who often talk to themselves, listen along to lectures, and record everything.
- Kinesthetic - Learners who are hands-on, think big picture, and take notes.

You might fit in one of these categories or a hybrid of these categories. The point is, by teaching yourself, you get to choose the medium that works best for your learning style.

No College or Bootcamp Needed

Many companies are starting to drop the 4-year degree requirement. Companies are even starting to hire individuals who may even go through a 3-6 month coding bootcamp. I don't think you personally need either of these. Much of what you're taught at college isn't practical to the workplace. Employers may expect you to reverse a linked list in an interview, but you'll unlikely have to do that on the job. On the other hand many of the career skills you're taught at a bootcamp you can learn on your own such as reading this book.

Practical Knowledge

As I hinted at earlier, you don't get practical knowledge from college or many bootcamps. Your preparation for the industry really comes down to doing things you would on the job. There is simply too much to learn and one of your superpowers today is having the choice of what you should learn. As you approach your self-taught journey, consider the 80/20 rule. What 20% of things should you learn will give you 80% of the results you're after? More on the 80/20 in a future chapter.

Portfolio Building

By working at your own pace, in your own style, and on practical things, you are building a portfolio of knowledge and projects that will help you when it comes time to apply for jobs of all kinds (full-time, freelancing, etc).

Embracing Life-long Learning

Having the motivation to regularly learn new skills will accelerate your career as a programmer. In a industry that can change what is trendy every couple years comes with it's own unique challenges. Learning about new things while also following your own curiosity will help you sustain your career without burning out.

🏆 On-Going

Constantly learning is the best thing you can do for yourself. Everyday that you get a little smarter is an opportunity for you to take one step closer to the goals in your life. Whether you ultimately decide to pick up programming or not is up to you, but getting into the habit of learning is something I hope you take away from this all.

☝ Voluntary

At this point you should either be feeling eager to get started or scared to death. These are normal feelings. When I got started on my learning journey, I knew absolutely nothing. I felt as if there were a physical cliff that I could look up and see just how much I have yet to learn to get my first job. This may make you feel like you should go do something else, but if you take the first step today like I did 10 years ago, I guarantee you will not regret it.

😄 Self-Motivated

Nobody is going to force you to learn. The only person who can motivate you at the end of the day is you. Although the present version of yourself might see teaching yourself to program to be intimidating & time-consuming, the future version of yourself will be thanking past you for getting started today.

✋ What This Book Is Not

Although this book is titled "Part-Time Programmer", this book will in fact not teach you how to program. Rather, this book's goal is to help you embrace a growth mindset, learn how to build new skills quickly, and guide you towards figuring out what you need to teach yourself.

⬛ Teach You How To Program

Because programming is quite opinionated and there's hundreds if not thousands of books that will teach you how to do basic things in a programming language, framework, or technology, this book's focus is on teaching you how to teach yourself, build learning habits & know what to learn to become a programmer faster.

🏆 Guarantee You Results

Only reading this book will not get you any results. You might leave this book knowing a few good tips as to getting into a better mindset, how to build a learning system, or maintaining your habits over time. If you choose to not apply anything that is in this book towards your everyday, then you're not going to see much change in your life. That's on you.

😨 Give You Unrealistic Expectations

This book is a very narrow minded opinion. I live in the USA, and the many reflections of this book are from my experience in the tech industry here. That means that your mileage may vary depending on if you're in another country. I do not sugarcoat my thoughts as to how you can be effective in the system or the amount of time it realistically takes to learn a new skill. You will get what you put into it and nothing more. Using this book can help you be smarter & work less when putting in that effort.

🎁 Provide Resources to Learn

Every minute, something in the tech industry becomes less relevant or outdated. Because of this, this book will not provide you with any resources as to what or how you should learn. Rather it is a book to give you the fundamentals as to how you use those resources you find. The resources I used to learn how to program would not hold up today, and so was the pattern with the resources before it.

Although many things may not change, people create new resources every single day that evolve how we learn as humans. I encourage you to find your own resources organically as they are typically the best resources available to you at the time. The world is huge and the internet and open source does a great job of curating the best resources known to us.

✅ Let's Get Started

With all of that out of the way, let's get started. It's not going to be an easy nor difficult journey, but it will be a long one. The earlier you get started, the closer you get towards your ultimate goals.

Homework #1 - Is Coding For Me?

By now you should have a good understanding of why you should consider learning programing, having your own personal reasons to code, and even the demand of software developers in the future. In this homework, I want you to ask yourself the following questions and write down your answers to them somewhere.

I'm the type of person who
_____.

The habit that will get me closer to being that person is
_____.

The easiest thing I can do today to start that habit is
_____.

CHAPTER TWO

Mindset

* * *

MINDSET

Elevate your thinking with the right mindset.

* * *

Learning How To Learn

The most beneficial thing you can do early in any career you pursue is to learn how to learn. What exactly does that mean? It means to be able to rapidly take on any new topic & be able to comprehend it in a short period of time. Many people stop learning after their formal education, but if you're reading this book, you can be in on a little secret. The secret is to never stop learning. Each new thing you learn in your everyday life can lead to opportunities bringing for success.

Unlearning Everything You Know

Before you can apply learning how to learn, you have to mentally prepare yourself by unlearning everything you think you know today. There's many things you were taught as a kid and even an adult that you may believe is true, but the reality is that our knowledge is always evolving. We're getting smarter every single day. What worked for us in the past does not necessarily mean it will work for us today. You were taught a specific way of learning while in school, and you might ask yourself whether there is a better way.

This is especially true in the tech industry. What worked for people 10 years ago is almost non-existent today. Programming languages & ecosystems have evolved with time, software development practices have gotten better, and the tools you're going to use have got smarter. So although you might think you can leverage what you know today, try your best to start from an empty slate and get in the habit of unlearning what no longer serves you.

Information Sponge

One of your main jobs is to become an information sponge for anything you're learning from books, courses, and others. The more that you can "unlearn", the more space there will be to absorb with. You're not only soaking in new information, but you're also following your curiosity to find the best answers you can.

Continue to be curious, ask questions every step along the way, and don't be afraid of inconveniencing somebody if you can absorb knowledge that you can then share with the world.

* * *

Learning Is Your Unique Advantage

Your unique advantage is learning. The faster & more you retain, the more likely you'll become an authority in the space. This can be at work, online, or even among your friends. Everyday is an opportunity to learn something new. Learning something new leads to opportunities. Those opportunities can lead to jobs, speaking gigs, recognition, and much more.

Better Ways To Learn

There are better ways to learn. Just like how our knowledge evolves over time, so does our learning techniques to help us retain more information and learn faster. Although we won't go into how until a later section, do know that what you know about learning something new today likely will differ from what you're going to learn about it.

Building Learning Habits

Depending on how you see it, a simple thing like reading a book for 30 minutes a night or working on a side project for an hour in the morning will have more impact on your developer journey than you may think. Getting into regular habits of learning new things will serve us more than anything in this book. Don't worry though, we're going to cover everything I know about habits in a future section so you can build these foundational learning habits.

New Ideas = New Opportunities

Every new idea you come across is an opportunity to apply it someway. You might read a book about a new software development process called "Extreme Programming (XP)" and you might convince your first boss the merits of it which leads to a more productive team & you then deserve all the credit. The point is, by learning how to learn & regularly getting into a habit of learning, you can use all the fresh ideas are opportunities that can benefit you in life.

Fast Brain, Slow Mind

Knowledge workers tend to have two different modes of thinking. A fast mode in which we're thinking faster than we can act, and a slow mode in which we're processing slowly to make our next moves.

* * *

🐇 Fast Brain

The fast brain is when you're primarily focused on accomplishing a single task & you may enter a state of flow to which your brain is working at a thousand miles per hour. Whenever you go into an intense study or work session where you look down at the clock after you're done and see hours have passed by although it felt like minutes. This is your fast mind doing work so fast that you lost your sense of time.

🐢Slow Mind

The slow brain is when you're more relaxed and subconscious is processing through a problem at it's own pace. Think back to the last time you went to bed or took a shower and suddenly had a eureka moment of solving a problem or having a brilliant idea. This is your slow mind doing work behind the scenes that you're not even aware of.

🤓Balancing Your Mind

Using too much of your fast brain can lead to burnout, and using too much of your slow mind can be unproductive. The key is to balance your mind with enough time each day to experience both the fast brain & slow mind. Many people may use focus sessions to get into fast brain mode, and then decompress after work to get into the slow mind.

As you may imagine, this doesn't work effectively for us all the time. We should rather employ our slow mind in a tactical way to have it work through new ideas & problems while we relax. We'll talk about employing workflows to help you do just that in a future section.

😨Limiting Beliefs

We were raised with a number of limiting beliefs about ourselves. These beliefs may hold you back from taking a risk, extending yourself a bit further, or even keeping you away from your dreams. Your limiting beliefs should not have a hold on you and before we move on, we're going to talk about them.

* * *

⏰Your past is not the present
Whatever beliefs you had about yourself in the past need to be acknowledged and understood. These beliefs that solidified when you were younger or in a more vulnerable mindset need to be challenged. You are not your past, and your past is not your future.

😄Positivity is prosperity
Limiting beliefs bring negativity in most cases. We hold onto these feelings of not being good enough, not accomplished enough, you name it. You can overcome this right now by bringing positivity into everything you do from now on.

Whenever a limiting belief comes up throughout your learning journey, you should smother it with positivity & make yourself feel empowered that you are overcoming it. Do not let your limiting beliefs to have a hold on your mental state. They will keep you grounded when you want to fly.

🧠Mind over matter
If you can master your mind, you can bring upon enough willpower to take action towards overcoming your limiting belief. Your actions speak louder than words, so when in doubt, take a small action or even a massive action towards your next learning goal. Keep in mind that your mental state dictates you taking action consistently, so being in the right mindset help you overcome.

⬆️Raise Your standards
You can raise your standards of your limiting beliefs by wanting more out of yourself. You get to set the bar as high or as low as you want, but I can guarantee that raising the bar & taking action everyday will show you that the limiting belief was a lie the whole time you kept telling yourself and you're the master of your own destiny.

🏃Challenge the status quo
The only way to overcome a limiting belief is to prove to yourself that what you thought was reality turned out to be false. Rather, with enough willpower & action you are able to challenge the status quo and show yourself that the silly existing belief you had was really not

that bad and you'll be empowered to do more that you thought you couldn't do before.

The Lies of Learning To Code

There are many lies that we tell ourselves before pursuing something that is challenging. For coding, there are many lies that prevent us from taking a step in learning. We're going to debunk many of those lies right now.

I'm not smart enough to become a programmer.

There's a misconception that programmers are really smart people. The reason why is because they can understand language & technology that not many people have taken the liberty to teach themselves. Most professional programmers are self-taught & learned from failing over and over by giving a computer instructions on what to do.

I'm not good at math and I heard programmers need to be good at it.

I know this may sound shocking, but many of the best programmers are not great at math. You may even ask a number of professionals in the industry who may tell you that they struggled through the math classes they had to take through university if they even went. You don't need to be good at math, and any math you will need can be learned before you need to use it.

I'm a slow learner and it will take forever to comprehend coding.

Many people who code professionally in the industry still have no idea what they are doing. Even those who have a good idea of what they are doing didn't get there until years working in the industry. Your comprehension comes with patience and perseverance.

I'm not going to remember much of what I'm learning.

Much of what we learn can become irrelevant in years or never used in a practical fashion. Many computer science degrees require advanced math & physics classes that are never used on the job. Just like math, you retain what you use on a everyday basis. If you learned something difficult in the past & never used it, the next time you learn something similar, you will already have a path making it easier to pick up.

* * *

It will take years before I'm good enough to get a job coding.

Plenty of entry-level & jr. programming jobs exist to the point where companies are more than willing to train you on the job & in-fact benefit from hiring you as early as possible (making them more money in the process). There is no such thing as being good enough to get a job coding. Many people can be good enough at building projects with code, but not great at interviewing and vice versa. Don't let time be a factor here, and if it is for you then you can accelerate that timeline by spending more time everyday on your learning journey.

I'm too old to change careers or learn something new.

You may have chose a career that you feel is a dead end or you're not growing enough in. You may even feel inspired and interested in technology now that it has taken over the world. Age is just a number, you can learn anything you set your mind on. Do not let previous careers, education, agism or other barriers prevent you from what you truly want. Get up and get after it.

The 80/20 Rule

There's one rule that I want you to keep in the back of your head that you'll keep asking yourself as you go about. That rule is known as the 80/20 rule or Pareto's principle.

The Pareto Principle

Simply stated, the Pareto principle is a rule suggesting that **20% of your activities will account for 80% of your results.**

This rule is helpful in your understanding of what will effectively move you forward in your journey and can be applied to any situation. Here's a few examples:

- What is the 20% of things I should learn to know 80% of what's asked in a job's requirements?
- What are the 20% of companies to apply to for 80% of the job interviews?
- What is the 20% of computer gear I need to do 80% of the learning today?

* * *

Constraining Yourself

You may notice that the Pareto principle in practice is setting a constraint. This is by design. The more that you focus your energy and attention towards overcoming the constraint, the more you speed up the process & make substantial progress.

Say you wanted to double your income today & your knew your best chance of doing that was to learn how to code. What type of constraints would you set on yourself to make that happen? We already covered a few ideas above, but say you wanted to do that in 6 months, how would you do it?

! Identifying Constraints

There may be existing constraints in your everyday life where you aren't following the 80/20 rule, but rather you're spending countless hours on things that feel unproductive. Your current job might feel like a constant challenge of surviving the 8 hour work day. This is a constraint that you will have until you can make substantial change. Is there something within the current constraint that can benefit a future constraint? Let's go back to the example of wanting to double your income in 6 months & learning to code was the path forward.

How could you take a step within your 8 hour work day to make 20% of the progress towards the 80% of that goal? That might be reading a programming break over lunch instead of going out with coworkers. That might be finishing your work early & running through programming tutorials online. Whatever it might be, keep the 80/20 rule in mind.

First Principles Thinking

Software engineering can be complex. Learning about it can be even more daunting. There's a concept of first principles thinking that you can keep in your mind whenever you are feeling overwhelmed or confused.

Path of least resistance

Humans are quite lazy. We tend to take the path of least resistance. Not sure how to approach a problem? You might google it. Not sure how to implement a feature? You jump on YouTube. Although these are great and natural things to be doing, keep in mind that we are not doing much thinking. We are letting other people who have solved these problems previously think for us.

Thinking for ourselves

There's many benefits for delaying the instant gratification of a solution online & simply thinking through things. The exercise of thinking and even getting into the regular habit of doing it will act as natural guide of following your unique understanding of the world. This challenges your current understanding with the reality that's understood by others. Majority of the time this is beneficial, especially as you just start out learning.

Start from the first basic truth

You can use the idea of first principles thinking by starting with the first basic truth that you understand. How you can get to that first basic truth is by continuing to ask yourself the question "why?". When you get to your first basic truth, you'll see that it tends to have a solid foundation & largely undisputed by others. Keep this in mind.

? Ask Why

Continuing to ask yourself the question of "why?" will help you get to the root of many things. It's like when a toddler is trying to get an understanding of the world & continues to ask you "why?". These help form our basic truths which is our fundamental understanding of how things work. You can typically break down complexity to a fundamental understanding simply by asking "why?".

If This Is True, Then What Else Is True?

Once you've established your fundamental understanding, you can then build upon it. In comedy improv, there is a concept of "Yes, And" which loosely translates to accepting the reality presented to you, and building upon it. Within engineering, we tend to think about logical truths. If you have already established your first basic truth, what else might be true? Building onto of your fundamental knowledge helps you make connections and establish patterns along the way.

* * *

Meta-Skills

When we think about skills, we tend to think of a full subject matter. For programming however, there are many meta-skills that will help you become better everyday. Investing time in each of these meta skills everyday will pay off substantially in the future.

Research Process

Programmers by nature are researchers. You are doing research to solve a problem by creating a solution for it. You may even establish hypotheses as to your understanding of the problem & even your solutions (your code).

You can have an organized strategy towards your research process with a few things:
- Having a centralized location to store information.
- Clearly articulating your problem.
- Gathering background information.
- Searching for the right terms.
- and many more

Everyone will have a different process towards how they research, but do know that it's important to think about your process as a system of inputs (problems, information, previous solutions) and it outputs your proposed solution.

Search Engines

A programmer is only as good as their ability to search. There are good ways to search, and there are bad ways to search. Going to google and just typing your search term is not always an effective way to search. Search engines are extremely powerful tools. Used right, they can serve you in ways others will think you're some computer genius.

Taking time to understand how to do advanced searches & the known syntax to do them is worth it's weight in gold. Looking for something on a specific website? There's an advanced term for that. Looking for something with a specific file extension? There's an advanced term for that. Take the time to understand the advanced side of search to make your searching effective.

33

* * *

GitHub Search

Similar to search engines, GitHub is one of the biggest code search engines in the world. They also have a concept of advanced search that can benefit you greatly. Want to find only popular code? There's a term for that. Want to find a recent example using a framework you're using? There's a term for that. Want to find an issue in a specific repository or owner of a library you're using? There's a term for that.

GitHub search slowly becomes your best friend once you realize that you can use it in unique ways beyond your typical search engine.

Touch Typing

Learning how to properly type can make a significant difference in your everyday work. Not only can you achieve speeds that you normally could not with hunt and pecking or whatever you might be doing today, but it's also the ergonomic option that your wrists and hands will thank you later.

Being able to type at a pace such as 50-80 wpm is a great start. With about ten minutes a day working on your typing speed & correctness, you can get up to over 100 wpm with high accuracy which adds up over your lifetime.

Keyboard Shortcuts

There are many keyboard shortcuts for your operating system of choice and the programs on that operating system. These keyboard shortcuts can save you time by not having to reach for a mouse or combines multiple steps into a single command.

Learning about the common shortcuts for the operating system you develop on & the shortcuts for your favorite IDE (integrated developer environment), code editor, and plethora of other tools is a good idea all around.

Vi/Vim & Emacs

If you want to take your touch typing & keyboard shortcut skills to the next level, you can enter the world of vi/vim & emacs or close alternatives. These are editors that are designed for the power user which focus on manipulating text & customization. These are tools for the productivity powerhouses in which you can remain inside an editor with only a keyboard and be able to do things like append at the end of a line, delete whole lines, match patterns, and navigate quickly through files.

These editors have steep learning curves, but with enough time invested each day, you can get down the basics to the point of using them effectively and incorporating them into your regular programming workflow.

Asking Questions

Being able to ask a good question can separate your problem solving abilities from others. One thing you might notice on a website like Stack Overflow or Quora is that good questions tend to have really good answers. To ask a good question, consider the following:

- Picture that you were being asked this question. Does it make sense?
- Imagine who you're asking only have a couple minutes to answer your question. How would you summarize your question to them?
- Pair your question with a title that represents the theme of your question.
- Less is more. Only include the minimum needed.
- What is the context? Communicate your goals & your environment.
- What have you tried? Go through a list of things you've tried already or found online.
- Show where you're stuck. Have a way that you can demonstrate your problem or share it.

Although you'll get better at asking questions with time, consider this as a skill you can work on everyday & get better at.

!? Problem Solving

There is a difference between problems and solutions. If you asked me, I'd say it's the following:

* * *

- A problem is a known unknown. It's our assumption that needs clarity.
- A solution is a known known. It's the facts we have from gaining clarity.

Being able to articulate a problem helps us gain clarity. A problem well-articulated is a problem that is mostly solved. Being able to communicate both a problem and a solution is how we gain clarity.

Additionally, to work on our problem solving ability, we can challenge ourselves with brain games, programming challenges, and even logic problems. One of my favorite things to do as a kid was buy workbooks of logic puzzles, cryptograms, and more. There's many apps that do this like brilliant, elevate, and luminosity to name a few.

Reading

Probably the most important skill is your ability to read & comprehend. I left it last as it should be emphasized as the one skill that you can work on every single day with as little as 30 minutes a day. You're going to be reading code, understanding that code, and putting it together as part of a larger context. You're also going to be reading through documentation, emails, specifications, and much more that your ability to read can accelerate or hinder your productivity.

You can even go as far as learning speed reading techniques to find the information you're seeking from the abundance of information we consume everyday as software developers. Your ability to read & search within what you're reading can help you comprehend more faster.

Playing To Your Strengths

No single person is born the same. Everyone has their own unique strengths and weaknesses that make them human. Focusing on your strengths is usually your best strategy, but keep in mind that you are only as strong as your weakest link.

No typical path

There's no typical path to becoming a software engineer. The closest you might have today is a traditional route of going through a 4-year degree program. Even then, it's becoming less and less prevalent today with the rise of self-taught & bootcamps.

Your path to becoming a developer will be unique compared to others. You may have went to college for a completely different specialization. You may have even had a past career in an industry not even related to software. Whatever it might be, just know that there's no typical path & that your path is unique.

Unique to your situation

Not everyone can afford college, bootcamps, or have a situation in which they can dedicate their full time & attention towards becoming a programmer. We have to make by with what is unique in our situation. That can be the 20 minutes between your classes, the lunch break you have for your shift, your morning or nightly routine, or even the dead time you may have when commuting or spending time with others.

We have to make due with what we have. Every minute counts towards your ultimate goal. That can mean making sacrifices of time to work on our goals. Although it may not be the most attractive option at the time, it can be the most rewarding.

Leverage your strengths

You're good at something. You might be good at building things. You might be good at researching things. You might even be good at solving problems. Whatever that might be, try to identify it early & use it towards your advantage. If you're good at building for example, you should take the opportunity to build. Do what you are exceptionally good at.

What makes you stand out

What will make you stand out from others is leveraging your strengths & unique situation. Everyone loves a good underdog story, so showing the adversity you've gone through can speak wonders & make you stand out like a weed. After all, the tallest weed tends to be the first noticed.

Your path is not going to be very linear. You're going to have many setbacks & overcome many challenges. So long as you are actively working on it every single day will make you stand out and speak for itself.

Elevating With Exercise & Eating Well

The mind is only as efficient as the body that supports it. There are a number of things you can do today to fuel your mind throughout the day & give yourself an edge as you're solving problems & learning new things.

Daily Movement

You may spend a lot of time sitting down. One way to change things up is to get up and go for a walk. There's been many studies and research that walking improves your problem solving ability & helps you think more creatively. Going for a 10-minute walk everyday benefits you in ways you may not see today, but as soon as you start doing it and seeing the benefits, you'll wish you had started sooner.

Elevated Heartrate

Although walking will make you less stagnant, a good goal is to elevate your heart rate with at least 30 minutes of exercise a day. Go on a run, play your favorite sport, or even lift some heavy objects. Whatever you choose to do, just try to make it a goal of elevating your heart rate to get the blood flowing throughout your body everyday. This will help you with your memory & retention.

Brain Foods

Our brain is only as good as the fuel we provide our bodies. There are many known brain foods out there like:

- Avocados
- Blueberries
- Broccoli
- Dark Chocolate
- Eggs
- Spinach
- Salmon
- Turmeric
- Walnuts

* * *

Finding what healthy foods you enjoy as snacks & main courses can help you learn faster. Do your research for what works best for your situation, but speaking from personal experience, as soon as I replaced fast food with regular brain foods, my knowledge exponentially grew.

🏋️ Running & Weightlifting

Although you may have an opinion on running or weightlifting, they are two of the most accessible and beneficial exercises available to you. Although I could go over the benefits each of these provide, I want you to consider another reason why you do these exercises, and that's to get out of your head.

What I mean by this is that it is healthy to regularly focus your attention on other things that are challenging. This helps kick our brain into that diffused mode of thinking where we are solving problems or processing things while doing something completely different. Running & weightlifting are no different, they serve as wonderful exercises to not only keep you in shape, but also help you work more efficiently. Find an exercise that ultimately grounds you, mine just happens to be running & weightlifting as you can do them by yourself.

📘 Homework #2 - Is My Mind Right?

By now you should have a good understanding of how we should embrace teaching ourselves new things with a fast brain/slow mind, overcome limiting beliefs, following the Pareto principle and slowly working on our meta-skills. In this homework, I want you to work on your daily routine and incorporate 3 different things that take under 30 minutes each to improve your mind & meta-skills.

Here's a small list for ideas that you can use:

- Go for a walk
- Eat a healthy meal
- Run a mile or two
- Pick up heavy weights and put them down
- Take a nap
- Try meditating and deep breathing
- Take a typing test

- Read a book
- Go to bed early
- Lookup your operating system's keyboard shortcuts
- Learn Google search syntax
- Ask a question on the internet
- Install Vim and learn how to exit it

CHAPTER THREE

System

* * *

**Thinking in systems with short
feedback loops.**

* * *

Becoming More Agile

In software engineering, there is a concept of being agile. This is typically used as a framework for building software that is valuable to customers very quickly. You can apply this to your learning journey by keeping these principles in mind as you are learning & as the industry introduces the latest and greatest tools & frameworks for you to use.

Fast and iterative

The heart of agile is it's ability to move fast at an iterative pace. What this means is that there is less overall planning & a focus on continuously iterating. Throughout your learning, you should keep this in mind. You want to move fast & focus on iterating to your next milestone of knowledge. You don't want to hold yourself back, rather you should feel at liberty to move on when you feel ready & iterate when needed.

Interactions over processes

Another key principle is the focus on interactions rather than long winded processes. For you organized folks out there like me, this is hard to let go, but do know it's worth it. Your interactions with what you are learning are much more important than your process of learning.

What does this mean exactly? Well this means that if you have an opportunity to apply the stuff you're learning to, you go and do it rather than make a process or plan to apply it.

Do things that work

Not everything that you do or learn will work out for you. You're going to fail a lot, and this is a good thing. When this happens, remember that you can always come back to what you know works for you. In fact, you should try to keep doing the things that work out best for you as they will help you move faster.

Respond to change

Having the ability to respond to change is what makes agile great. By the end of an iteration, we tend to become smarter & wiser as to what we should do next. If we simply just did what was next on the list, we might be missing out on some organic discoveries that come from our natural curiosity and newly found understanding.

This should encourage you to at anytime make changes within your learning journey that you believe will best suit you. If you find yourself wasting too much time in one area or not understanding, then simply move on and come back to it later.

Getting Stuff Done With Scrum

Scrum is one of two implementations of agile that we'll cover. It keeps the principles of agile to heart while also providing you a practical way to go about organizing your tasks, time, and energy in an effective way.

Backlogs as a to-do list

Based on a large to-do list known as a backlog, scrum lives and breathes from a centralized backlog of glorified to-do items. Your backlog is your ultimate sense of truth. It's how you see the world in terms of what tasks you need to take on with priorities defined as you're able to groom through the backlog in future iterations.

It can be comprised of small tasks or even larger projects that are made up of tasks on your backlog. Each item on your backlog can be managed by you. You can provide as much or as little information as you'd like for future you to understand. Additionally, you can provide different states of the items on your backlog such as if it's waiting for something, blocked on something, or even the perceived priority of the item in comparison to others usually using a P0-P3 scale where p0 = the most important and should be done as soon as possible.

Bite-sized Pieces

Each task in the backlog needs to be broken down to a bite-sized piece that you can take on easily during an iteration. Software engineers get extremely good at taking complex things and breaking them down into simpler ones.

For every task on your backlog, you should be able to break it up into bite-sized pieces depending on your preference of working such as taking hours, days, or weeks.

T-Shirt Costing

Many projects on your backlog will need loose estimations to ensure that you don't spend too much time on them. There's a concept in software engineering called T-Shirt costing in which estimates for projects are given a shirt size like S, M, L, XL to provide how many weeks it might take to complete.

- Small - 0-2 Weeks
- Medium - 2-4 Weeks
- Large - 4-8 Weeks
- X-Large - 8-16 Weeks

You can use whatever estimations you want or even take on your own fun way of estimating how long it might take you to do a task or project.

Sprints before Marathons

Iterating in scrum is usually done in what are known as sprints. These sprints are defined as a number of weeks in your iteration. To move faster & be more responsive to change, you might have 2-week long sprints. For more stability & reflection at the end, you might have 4-week long sprints(also known as monthly).

Now that you have your personal sprint defined with a number of weeks, you can now get to work & kick-off your first ceremonies.

Regular Ceremonies

There are 3-4 regular scrum ceremonies depending on how you do it. One to plan, one to review, one to retrospect, and one regularly to check in.

Sprint Planning

Planning is by far your most important scrum ceremony. Usually on the last week before a new sprint starts, you'll do what's known as a sprint planning. This is where you can plan your sprint based on how much capacity you'll have that sprint. For personal sprints, this is going to be more of an exercise of trial & error.

Although you'll eventually get the grasp for how you might cost each task & project on your backlog, estimation in software is not an exact science & don't hold yourself too accountable for finishing early or missing estimated deadlines.

During the sprint planning, you will review your backlog by going through each item based on it's perceived priority or previously-defined priority. You'll then assign each item to a person, in this case that will be you. Try to follow the less is more idea when it comes down to personal sprints.

Daily Standup or Weekly Sit-downs

Everyday or every week you should check in with yourself to see how you are progressing. The most popular way to do this is by doing what's known as a daily standup. This is where you spend up to 15 minutes to check in with yourself and ask the following questions:

1. What did you do yesterday?
2. What will you do today?
3. What's in your way?

As you may imagine, this is extremely helpful on a day to day basis as it helps bring clarity into what you're doing, why you're doing it, and how you can proceed or find a way to get unblocked if needed.

The other format is the weekly sit-down. It's very similar to the daily standup except that you do it once a week rather than everyday. These are typically longer sit-downs to account for everyday in the week. You can spend as little as 15 minutes in a sit-down or up to 60 minutes so that you can ensure your next week will go all according to plan.

Sprint Review & Retrospectives

Reviewing your iterations and being able to have a retrospective of what went well, what didn't go so well, and what you're going to start doing in the future is what reviews & retrospectives are all about. These are usually lumped into a single ceremony, but can also be broken into two separate ceremonies depending on your preference.

* * *

The sprint review focuses on going through your planned sprint items & reporting the statuses of each. Did you complete them? How much more work is left on them? Are there any major blockers?

The sprint retrospective on the other hand is a chance to think critically about the last sprint. What were some of the challenges you had last sprint? Was some of the work too difficult? Did you not have enough to do? Were there any challenges or learnings from the last sprint that you should take on to the next? This is a great opportunity to adjust your process to make your next sprint even more successful.

Celebrating Milestones

Most importantly, you should celebrate the milestones you accomplish through your sprints. These celebrations can be as simple as being a little smarter than you were the previous sprint or as large as wrapping up a project. If you make an effort to celebrate your wins, you'll get into a habit of doing great work throughout your sprints. I'm cheering for you, so get started!

Personal Kanban

Kanban is the second of two agile implementations we'll cover. It's based on the Japanese word for billboard & is a more visual system to help you understand how to balance your efforts, understand your capacity, and spot bottlenecks easily.

Physical or Digital Boards

To start with Kanban, you need a board. The board can be a physical board like a wall or even a piece of paper on a desk. It can also be a digital board using one of the many software services that offer a kanban approach like Trello, Jira, and Todoist.

The boards are separated into equal sized columns that visually represent a status or category of work. Next, cards are placed under their respective column until they are worked on. As you progress, the cards will make it's way through the kanban board & eventually removed from the board itself.

* * *

🎴 Visual Cards

The most visual aspect of the kanban board are the individual cards. These are typically sticky notes if you're doing a physical kanban board. The most important piece of information on a card is the title. The cards also have status signals that help you understand how they are logically categorized. Most of the time that represents a way to see who is working on it, within what context it should be worked on, when it's due, and a description or other attachments that will help when the card is picked up.

✅ To Do, In Progress, Complete

The least amount of columns a kanban board should have is around 3 (to do, in progress, and complete). Many digital kanban boards will default to these three columns, but you can set it up to your preference & working style. The most important part with columns is to have a visual way to understand what state of work the card is in.

As you may imagine, your backlog would live in the "to do" column & you can continuously add to the column. The "in progress" column is to show that you're actively working on the item and will either complete it or abandon it after working on it. Lastly, if you do complete the item, you might then move the card over to "complete".

🐶 Work In Progress Limits

One of the benefits of kanban is the visual representation of knowing how much capacity you have at a quick glance. You might look to the "in progress" column and see more tasks under it than a single person can handle. This is where a work in progress limit comes into play. You can set a realistic guideline to your kanban board in which you only allow a maximum number of cards under a column at a time. For the "in progress" example, you might set a limit of 3 cards to ensure you aren't biting off more than you can chew. This helps you limit your resources & pushes you to focus more on the work than the planning.

😀 Reasons for Kanban

There are two main reasons you should use kanban. The ability to limit your work in progress, and one of the best ways to visualize your work. Your kanban board should be very simple & straightforward. It shouldn't add too many rules or complexity or it becomes unmanageable. Try starting with a physical kanban board on your wall or desk & when you feel like you have the hang of it, move onto a digital format that is more powerful to your liking. Good luck!

Your Learning System

One thing programmers do better than others is their ability to think in systems. In other words, if I provide some kind of input, what is the output of it? This is a powerful way to think because we can think in terms of a personalized learning system. What are the inputs that go into your learning system, and what outputs are the result of your great work?

Thinking In Systems

There are many elements to a system. These elements tend to have some type of connection to each other & interact together to achieve something. As they achieve things, you are provided artifacts as to how the system overall behaves. There's a **stock** which is an observable aspect of your system such as seeing how much time you spent into learning. There's also a **flow** in which you can see if a stock changes with different elements of the system. When this is repeated, you create what's known as a feedback loop because there is now a change of the stock based on the flow for it.

What does that mean in simpler words though? It means that you can understand the elements of your system better by seeing it from a 1000 ft view and experimenting with it.

Inputs and Outputs

To think of your system in simpler terms, just consider the words inputs and outputs. You may put an input into an element of your system and there is an output. You can also think of this as a function. You put inputs into your function, and your function may or may not return some type of output.

As you may imagine, as you see the outputs of the various things you put into your system, you're going to tweak them to your liking. One thing to consider though is when your system does not show any type of output, it may be a sign of a sunk cost or it has potential to provide an even greater output in the future.

One example might be learning data structures & algorithms. Imagine you go to a job interview, prepared for the interview by grinding DS&A questions only to be surprised that they only care about your practical knowledge. All that time spent was all for nothing! Or was it? Maybe months or years down the line, you are tasked with a problem that requires your DS&A knowledge and you see a solution because it's familiar.

Bottlenecks

A huge benefit of thinking in systems with inputs & outputs is the ability to identify bottlenecks in our everyday processes. You are going to get stuck, and being able to understand what is causing the bottleneck is more important than the temporary confusion or not grasping a concept. When you identify a bottleneck, you are acknowledging a weakness & can come up with a plan to strengthen it.

For many, a bottleneck is whiteboard interviews. It's something you're never going to learn in college, bootcamps, or even teaching yourself until you actually apply for a job. One of the main bottlenecks is knowing concepts like Big-O notation to assess the time complexity of a function. By seeing this as a weakness in your whiteboard interviewing abilities, you can then come up with a plan to learn Big-O notation to make it one of your strengths instead.

Interconnectedness

Outside of inputs & outputs or elements in our system, thinking about the system as a whole is fundamental to systems thinking. Every hour you spend on learning, every google search you make, and even the time spent on snacking can have some type of influence on your overall system.

Each element is reliant on other elements. Your brain needs fuel to learn, your learning needs good resources, and those good resources need to be applied. Every element is connected, and seeing how they are connected will make you more effective.

* * *

Synthesis

When you combine two or more elements of your system together, you get what's known as synthesis. Synthesis gives us an understanding of the whole & the individual parts of our system. We can then understand each element's relationship with each other and the dynamics of the whole system. This helps you see the interconnectedness of your system.

The inputs of reading books about a programming language will result in outputs of have functional knowledge of programming. The inputs of regular hour long code sessions will result in outputs of working code. Each of these outputs represents another connection & opportunity. That functional knowledge of programming & working code demonstrates your ability to do a job professionally. By now, you might see the pattern. The more that we see our system as combined elements, the more we can focus on our bottlenecks and have more autonomy with our strengths.

Emergence

The synergies of our system result in outcomes. Those outcomes can be experience, knowledge, job opportunities, or even apps on the App Store. Great things will emerge from an optimized system. These are the natural outcomes that come from putting in the inputs in an effective & unique way that works for you.

Feedback Loops

As everything is interconnected & synergies become more apparent, you will start to receive feedback from the connected elements in your system. This is known as a feedback loop. Feedback loops help you understand the overall efficiency or inefficiency within your system. These feedback loops can be both positive or negative. A negative feedback loop if not managed, will turn into a bottleneck. A good feedback loop will turn into a positive outcome. Your natural goal with feedback loops are to balance them to the best of your ability.

Here's an example. You decide that going to the gym straight after your work shift helps you get into the get shit done mindset. The input here is going to the gym. Doing so, puts you into a state of accomplishment throughout the rest of the night. This empowers you to crack open your laptop & resume a coding tutorial until you get too tired & you decide to then go to bed.

This is a positive feedback loop because you are incentivizing your habit of learning to code by pairing it with another element of your system. More on habits in a later chapter.

Causality
When your feedback loops give you a positive or negative outcome, this is known as causality. This is great because we can now use our debugging skills to understand what elements & relationships within our system caused the positive or negative feedback loop, and we can either double down on it, or replace it with something better.

Homework #3 - Create Your System
By now you should have a good understanding of the concept of agile, two implementations of agile such as scrum & kanban, and how to think in terms of a learning system. Now is your chance to create your own learning system by choosing an implementation and starting to create a backlog for where you'll track what you'll learn and set due dates or priorities on them until they are done.

Here's what you should do:

1. Choose an agile implementation such as scrum or kanban. Read up more about them too!
2. Find a resource online like trello, asana, notion, and many others for a digital solution or create your own tracker on paper to manage your backlog of tasks.
3. Schedule your first iteration by coming up with 3 items to work on (if kanban) or plan your weeks out (if scrum).
4. Iterate on your tasks until completed (if kanban) or work on completing your tasks until the sprint is over (if scrum).
5. Review your progress daily, weekly, and monthly. Have a sprint review when the sprint ends (if scrum).
6. Repeat #3-5

Note: If you don't really care to add this much process to your learning journey, then come up with your own system that works for you!

CHAPTER FOUR

Roadmap

* * *

ROADMAP

How to become the cartographer.

* * *

Knowing What To Learn

To make the most of your time, you will need to know what to learn. Here's the thing, nobody is going to be able to tell you exactly what you need to know before you're going to be ready for a job or project. Everyone out there is doing their best with the information they have on hand. Colleges may give you a completely different roadmap than a bootcamp might. And your own personal roadmap may drastically differ from a bootcamp.

Free Doesn't Mean Good

There are many free resources out there that will tell you what you should learn. These can be amazing resources that a single person or a whole community puts together and maintains. There can however also be many resources out there that aren't put together well nor maintained. Just because something is free, does not necessarily mean it is good. When you're going through resources, use a few things as proxies to determine if it's good or not. Here's a few ideas:

- GitHub Stars - How many people are following the resource on GitHub.
- Popularity on Google - Does it come up on the first page with various searches?
- Reviews or Perspectives - What have people been saying about it?
- Commonality to Known Resources - Does it include popular resources already that are known to be good?

Transparency Helps

One of my biggest problems with learning & making a decision on what to learn is that many of the institutions that promise to prepare you for a job do not publish their curriculums to the public. Sure they may give you a good idea based on the class names or the topics covered, but they don't go into depth unless you do the research yourself. Any resource that is transparent and lets you know up front what you're signing up for is a winner in my book. There shouldn't be any surprises or doubts of why you're learning something.

* * *

Needle In The Haystack

Sometimes the best resources are the ones we find on our own. There are many amazing blogs, videos, and even full courses out there on the internet that have never been picked up formally by others because it didn't win the PageRank algorithm. You're going to come across a number of resources in your journey that are invaluable. When you come across these, make sure to store them somewhere so you can pay it forward to the next person when you share your learning journey.

Degrees for Free

You can get a computer science degree online for free, did you know that? No, you will not receive a piece of paper in return, but you will get the same knowledge and in most cases, an in-depth understanding of the topics compared to an average college graduate. This takes a little work on your end to first setup, but it can be well worth it.

Open Source Degrees

There are a number of open source computer science degrees that the community has put together that include a whole curriculum with links to each course on a MOOC platform like Coursera, edX, Udacity, and more. These open source degrees are wonderful to help supplement your practical knowledge of programming. Sometimes they can be a bit overkill as it's not often you'll need to use the maths or theory included in them.

DIY Degrees

Another option of a free degree is to do it yourself. Here's how you might do that. Go find the curriculum of your favorite or dream school that offers the program of choice (in this case computer science). Next, look for a detailed breakdown of every class required to obtain the 4-year bachelor's degree. Now, google or find the syllabus online for a previous iteration of the class, you should be able to understand what book was used, what topics were and weren't covered, and even how long the course will be. Finally, you can pickup the book, go through the chapters & exercises on that topic, and get started learning.

You might think this is a huge waste of time if you're not actively enrolled in college & receiving the credit, but in many cases this can be some of the best self-study you can do as it really challenges you to teach yourself. Much of the time, the professors of these classes have their whole course syllabus & supplemental resources online on their website or department webpage for anyone to download (lectures included sometimes too).

Developer Roadmaps

For more practical knowledge, there are what's known as developer roadmaps on the internet. These are somewhat like college syllabuses in that they give you a list of things you should know on the road towards becoming a developer.

Open Source Roadmaps

The open source community does a great job of putting together roadmaps for various different technology stacks of developer disciplines. These open source roadmaps are typically updated as the industry starts to shift in direction.

For example, if you wanted to be a full-stack developer, you might find a full-stack roadmap. That roadmap is going to cover many different topics like the internet, HTML, CSS, JavaScript, Version Control, Package Managers, Build Tools, JavaScript Libraries/Frameworks, DOM, APIs, and much more.

These roadmaps help give you the high-level view of the general things to learn. These roadmaps do not typically go into depth & sometimes that can be challenging as knowing "how much HTML" to learn is just as important. This is where using your best judgement will help you. Only you can make the judgement call of whether or not you're ready to move on to the next topic. Keeping in mind the 80/20 rule, you only need to know the 20% of a topic that does 80% of the things you'll do with it.

Some developer roadmaps can become outdated very quickly if they are not maintained. Tech moves extremely fast. Within a couple years, you might be learning a completely new programming language or framework that a type of development relies on. Don't be alarmed though, this is usually the evolution of these ecosystems that took many years to get to the point of switching & now you're on the bleeding edge.

Bootcamp Curriculums

Another way to get an idea of what you should learn is to go find a bootcamp curriculum online or even ask for a syllabus by reaching out to one you might be interested in. Majority of the time these bootcamps will post a syllabus online for those to view. This will help give you an opinion on what type of stack they are teaching and you can compare that to the industry or what you're seeing on open source roadmaps.

Some bootcamps might teach a language you're not interested in like Ruby. Although you can't knock it till you try it, you might even do more research to see if Ruby developers are in demand in your local area. It's very possible there's less Ruby developers than Java developers and perhaps you might need to consider swapping out certain parts of your roadmap with things you're personally interested in.

The point is, although you might not get a deep roadmap for what a bootcamp is covered, you can at least get a high level one and how many weeks they spend on each topic before moving on. This can help you understand a general timeframe of how long you should spend in each area as well.

Reverse Engineer Your Dream Job

Your dream job may seem like it's unattainable at first. You look at the job requirements & suddenly feel like you will never be qualified or it will take many years to get to the point of being qualified. This is where you can use what you learned previously to now reverse engineer your dream job.

Finding Your Dream Job

Finding your dream job opportunity through a job posting is a great place to start. This will help you get a solid understanding of what you need to learn to be a qualified candidate for the position. Many dream jobs may have qualifications that seem excessively difficult that a single person could qualify, and that's for good purpose. It's mostly to provide a standard baseline as for the type of candidates that the company would like to hire for the job.

This shouldn't deter you however. In fact, it should motivate you to work everyday towards each of those requirements and build the leverage so when another position opens up, you're more than qualified for the job and what it may entail.

Characteristics of a Dream Company

Don't worry so much as to the exact position, worry more about what the company culture is surrounding the position. Is it a job where you will feel happy? Will you feel like although you qualify for the work, you aren't overworking yourself to unhappiness? How does the company feel about the growth of their employees? Do they actively invest towards your future education?

Keep all of these characteristics in mind when you're searching for a dream job. The dream job can be in multiple companies, but you will need to ensure that you find a company that ultimately fits with your personal values.

What you really should care about is what is the skillset required to land the job at any of these dream companies?

Follow The Trend

When in doubt, you can always follow the trends in the industry. Programming languages, frameworks, and even certain technology can become trendy from time to time. There will always be popular things to learn. There are advantages and disadvantages to this though.

Only Learning What's Cool

People typically follow the trends. They might see a lot of traction around a given framework & decide to pick it up. What's most understood about these trends is that many people get stuck in the thinking that the trendy thing is "the best way" to do something. If you were to ask any person who has been in the industry long enough, they will tell you that these things come and go.

This can even create a divisiveness to where you'll hear people yell loudly that only one thing can be good in a world of many. You don't want to get caught in the trends in the sense of tribalism. You want to ensure you are following the trend because it has momentum & opportunities compared to others.

Two Groups of People

For things that are trendy, you're going to come across two main groups of people. First is the people who think the trendy thing is going to become the next big thing. Second is the people who think the trendy thing is going to help innovate the next big thing.

Although you may even see extreme personalities such as those who hate the latest & greatest trend, this isn't very productive as the reason something is trendy is the fact that it has popularity & momentum in the ecosystem.

? Developer Surveys

There are many yearly developer surveys that help you understand what is trendy today. Some surveys like Stack Overflow Developer Survey, HackerRank Developer Skills, and even SlashData State of the Developer Nation can be great resources to help you see what people are learning, what they enjoy using, and what they plan to learn in the future.

New Job Postings

Another method is to look at some upcoming startups or companies & the type of developer jobs they are posting for. You'll see certain technology choices in the requirements that may match with the developer surveys or what you may already know from being involved in the developer ecosystem.

What You Like

You should follow a simple rule at the end of the day. That rule is to learn & use what you like. If you enjoy building mobile applications with a specific framework, then use it! If you had a great experience building a game with a certain game engine, then use that! Don't follow trends simply because they are popular right now. You may worry about the feeling of missing out, but do know that it doesn't ultimately matter so long as you enjoy it & can find work doing what you enjoy.

* * *

Homework #4 - Build A Roadmap

By now you should have a decent idea of the type of resources that are out there in the world to take advantage of. Whether you go down the route of more theory-based learning such as following a CS degree's curriculum, or whether you go down the route of more practical-based learning such as a developer or bootcamp roadmap.

Here's what you should do:

1. Do your research on what programming language and frameworks make sense to start learning. Use developer surveys, jobs in your area, and trends to help you understand your options.
2. Choose your path of learning of more theory or learning more practical skills. You can always come back to these based on your goals at a future date.
3. The path you choose should have at least one primary programming language you will be learning such as Java, JavaScript, Python, C#, and others. Make sure your path matches your research!
4. Start to dissect your chosen path's roadmap by adding bite-sized tasks of what you need to learn to your learning system's backlog. By bite-sized, this means nothing that will take more than a couple days maximum. The more specific the better.
5. Plan out the next 3 months today and work towards the next 6 months if you can. 3 months is good enough to start with as we got to remember to respond to change!

CHAPTER FIVE

Habits

* * *

HABITS

What you repeatedly do, you become.

* * *

🫥 Habits To Shape Your Future Self

As we start thinking about our habits, I want you to think about how these habits will help shape the future you. Who do you want to be? Where do you want to be in 1 year? 5 years? 10 years? Your destiny is in your hands and the system of habits you create.

🗿 Identity Based Habits

If you're having trouble determining how a habit fits into your life, ask yourself "Does this habit help me become the type of person I aspire to become?"

There is a mighty fine power of delayed gratification that will come into the light as you continuously work on your habits.

Think about it...

- If you delay the gratification of getting fast food, you'll eat healthier when you get home.
- If you delay the gratification of watching Netflix instead of working on your side project, you'll launch a product sooner.
- If you delay the gratification of scrolling Facebook instead of studying for your final, you'll ace your test.

➡️ Delayed Gratification

If you want to be successful, at some point you will need to learn how to be disciplined and take direct action instead of getting distracted and falling back to things that are easy. You have to ignore the things that are easy in favor of doing something harder.

You have to start thinking like future you. Dress like the future you would. Execute on a routine like the future you would have.

🎯 Systems vs. Goals

You've heard the timeless wisdom that in order to get something we want in life, we must set specific, actionable goals. You may have even heard this be called SMART goals (Specific, Measurable, Achievable,

Relevant, Time-constrained).

Why SMART is dumb

I approached my habits this way for many years. Everything I did in life was a specific SMART goal. Whether that was to do well in school, learn how to program, or balance my work and life.

Here's the thing, I failed at pretty much each of these goals because I had a terrible system behind each one of them. I would let procrastination kick in daily, and my motivation levels were the lowest ever. Sure my goals were eventually reached, but it took longer than it really should have to do better in school, learn to build a mobile app, and spend more time with my family.

Your System of Learning

Think about it, if you wanted to do well in school, it revolves around your system of studying. If you wanted to build a mobile application, it revolves around your system of learning to code, developing features, and squashing bugs.

And if you wanted to spend more time with your family, it revolves around your system of optimizing your work schedule, scheduling your extra curriculars, and much more.

Now the question I want to ask you is...**What if we ignored goals all-together and focused on systems instead?**

Results are Outputs of your System

Instead of worrying about the end result, the results would come naturally because you're so honed in on the system rather than the end-goal. You could argue that the end-goal is the driving force to improve the system which gives even more fire power to why the system is so important.

Even with ambitious goals, what ultimately matters is the system underneath. If you wanted to become the next CEO, CTO, etc of a company, it's not going to be your ambitious goals that sets you apart from the others. It's going to be your **deliberate focus to improve your system to get shit done.**

* * *

When you achieve a goal, it's a momentary feeling. You may have been promoted, but what next? Do you plan to stay at that level for the rest of your career? Or will you improve your system to reach the next level? This is what is referred to being so good that they can't ignore you.

I also want to paint another picture here, what if you don't reach your goal? Or what happens if the satisfaction you thought you'd have from obtaining your goal actually isn't all what you thought it would be? Goals restrict yourself to thinking of best-case / worst-case scenarios. You're focused more on the end-result rather than actually doing.

Goals for Direction, System for Doing

A system in this case takes your mind off these feelings that can leave you unmotivated. Instead you will learn to trust your own process instead of comparing yourself to your achievements.

I'm not saying that goals are not important, but they are the by-product of a great system. Having goals are ultimately great for planning and focusing what you want to do with your life, but by no measure should they be your end-all, be-all when it comes to creating a system. Goals will provide you the direction you need as you navigate life and even push you forward in the short-term. Systems will provide you the process you need to incrementally push yourself forward in the long-term.

How Habits Work

Have you ever wondered how habits work? I know I didn't care until I changed my habits drastically. Going from being a night owl, to a morning person did not happen overnight. It did however allow me to become much more productive than I ever was before. This is because I learned about basic patterns that habits follow.

No Secret Formula

The difficult thing about habits is that there's no secret formula to quickly change habits or develop new ones overnight. They take time, and consistency. Good habits are driven by strong cravings. If we have the desire to do better in our personal and work lives, we have a desire to be better than we were yesterday.

* * *

Success is the product of habit and deliberate practice. There are many habit theories out there, and you can find what works best for your life, but what matters is **learning the skills of habit-building and habit-breaking so one can adopt the right set of habits for a period of time.**

2 BJ Fogg's Habit Loop

Take for example the following sentence, **these habits work based on a two-step pattern**: "After I <Cue>, I will <Routine>." This is a very simple definition of a habit.

After a cue, you perform a routine. This is a very powerful tool as one can then chain many habits together like the following:

- After I wake up in the morning, I will read one chapter of Code Complete.
- After I read, I will workout at the gym.
- After I workout, I will take a shower.

Simplified, this can look like:

- After I 🛏, I will 📖
- After I 📖, I will 🏋
- After I 🏋, I will 🚿

You get the point. For some people this system of habits works for them. However for other people, there is something missing such as a reward.

3 Charles Duhigg's Habit Loop

These habits work based on a **three-step pattern**:

1. Cue - A thing said or done that serves as a suggestion to perform the habit.
2. Routine - A behavior you engage in.
3. Reward - The recognition of the habit being completed.

* * *

The reward is the source of satisfaction that makes the habit easy to repeat. This can be as small as smelling a cup of coffee, to allotting yourself a cheat meal in the day.

4 James Clear's Habit Loop

These habits work based on a **four-step pattern**:

1. **Cue** - A thing said or done that serves as a suggestion to you that there's a reward to be found.
2. **Craving** - A powerful desire to change something to get the reward.
3. **Response** - A thought or action one takes to obtain the reward.
4. **Reward** - The feeling of satisfaction or dissatisfaction of whether you should perform the habit again or not.

In this book, we'll be using both BJ Fogg & James Clear's work on habits as the basis for what works well.

The Power of Compounding

There's a power to doing the same thing day-in and day-out. That power is consistency which in-turn compounds after each day you successfully put in a repetition. If you're able to put in the work every single day to get 1% better, you'll be ~38% better after 365 days. It's all about the inputs, environment, and behaviors you choose to get better each day.

Inputs

Your brain & body act like a fine-tuned system. The inputs you put into your body will in-turn give you an output. That output could be good, or it could be bad. If you choose give your brain constant inputs like television shows, video games, and other inputs that make you feel good in the moment, you'll probably not see much value over a year. Think of it in another way, what if you changed those inputs to be things that taught you something new each day? What if you substituted   television shows with reading or video games with working on a side project? Where do you think you'd be in a years time?

This is no different than your physical body. If you put in the time to workout or eat healthy every single day for a year, you're bound to see results. The best way to think about this is that the garbage you put into your system will result in garbage out. How might you instead put value into your system and in result have value as an output?

Environment

You are the average of the people you hang around with, the environment you're in, and the activities that you partake in. In the spirit of compounding and becoming better everyday, you should challenge yourself with surrounding yourself around people, surroundings, and things that excite you to become better.

Go find people who are doing the things that you want to be doing. Go to events where people are building the things you want to be building. And most importantly, surround yourself with the things that excite you.

Behaviors

What you do is ultimately who you become. Each behavior models your future identity. Changing your behaviors can be hard, but ultimately rewarding. Having behaviors that serve you or produce value in some way is how you compound over time. Improving your behaviors day in and day out will help you in the long run. Keep an eye on your behaviors & check in with yourself regularly to ensure that your behaviors are serving you, and you're not the one serving them.

Debugging Habits

Knowing what you do every single day and why you do it can be an extremely valuable practice. Your system is only as good as your daily habits & sometimes we can fall back into habits that don't provide us much value. When we become aware of these, we can find the root cause and bring our habits back to serve us.

Ability, Motivation, and Prompt

There are three main things that will help you debug your habits on a daily basis. Those three things are having the ability to do something, the motivation to do something, and a trigger moment in which you do the thing or you don't.

Majority of the time you will have the ability to do something, but not the motivation to do it. Motivation is quite fickle, it can come and go & it's extremely hard to sustain.

Whenever you find yourself not doing a habit that you believe is beneficial for you, ask yourself the following questions:

- Am I motivated enough to do it?
- Do I have the ability to do it?
- Is there a prompt telling me to do it?

If you find yourself saying no to any or many of these questions, you'll know exactly how you can in-fact change yourself to do the habit instead. Not motivated? Don't rely on it, rely on the ability or prompt instead. No ability? Use your motivation or prompt instead. No prompt? Well now you have problems because even with motivation or ability, you have nothing to let you know to do it. So when you notice this, take time to create a prompt!

Momentum is Motivation

The easiest way to sustain motivation is to have momentum behind it. Building momentum is quite challenging however & takes time to build up. As you successfully do something, you build momentum to be able to do it again. Being able to ride the momentum you build is how you can sustain motivation over a long period of time. You cannot rely on motivation alone however. You'll never be constantly inspired to do something unless you've already built the momentum to continuously do it. Each repetition that you put in to build the momentum will make it extremely hard to not have enough ability and motivation to in-turn accomplish.

Behavior Equation

There's an equation that you can use to understand how any of your behaviors come to life. That equation can help you understand why you do the certain things you do, and how you might be able to debug your behaviors when they go awry.

B = MAP

Your behaviors are based on three main factors. Your motivation, your ability, and a prompt to do something. You can have little motivation, but high ability & still do something. You can have high motivation, but little ability & still do something. You can have some motivation, and some ability & still do something. Understanding that your behaviors come from this simple equation can help serve you in the long run.

Brainstorming Behaviors

You probably have a list of the behaviors you do every single day as part of your routine. These are the behaviors that you've picked up over your lifetime & they serve you in some unique way today.

Taking some time to list out these behaviors can be quite useful to help you understand why you do what you do. One such way of doing this is to grab a piece of paper & a pencil or even open a text editor to type out your behaviors as they come to you.

Take 10 minutes right now to list out all of your behaviors that you do in a regular day. Think through just about everything from what you do when you first wake up to what you do when you shut your eyes for bed. Walk yourself through a typical day & get a rough idea of what you might be doing at a certain time in the day.

Now that you have a list of behaviors that you already do, take another 10 minutes to brainstorm behaviors that will serve you towards your journey of learning how to program. Think about everything that you may need to do in order to be successful in doing so.

Combining Behaviors

Now that you have two lists of behaviors, one in which goes through your current behaviors, and one in which goes through behaviors you believe will help you be successful in learning how to program, now it's time to combine your behaviors.

* * *

71

Start by circling or marking each behavior from your current behavior which serves you in some way (happiness, value, or even just because). Remove any behaviors that don't actively serve you today & find a way to replace those with behaviors from the list that you just wrote down that will make you successful.

●●Making Habits Obvious

Habits that are obvious are the ones that are obvious enough to do. You can make your habits more obvious by scoring your habits today, providing a context like when and where, stacking your habits that make sense, designing your environment to work for you, and reducing your exposure to the big time wasters.

✚Habit Scorecard

Before you can create new habits, you need to understand your current habits. One of the greatest challenges in changing habits is maintaining awareness of what we're actually doing day-by-day. Without knowing, it's very easy for bad habits to take over.

The more automatic a behavior becomes, the less likely we will actually think about it in a positive or negative fashion. Instead we think of it as something that we just do rather than how it impacts our future.

First, we're going to go through everything we do in a day and create a list. Here's a list that you might create right now:

- Wake up
- Turn off alarm
- Check notification on phone
- Go to the bathroom
- Take a shower
- Get dressed
- Make breakfast
- Leave for work
- etc

Once you have done this for your entire day, you will analyze each behavior and ask yourself:

* * *

- Is this a good habit? Put a "+" next to it.
- Is this a bad habit? Put a "-" next to it.
- Is this a passive habit? Put a "=" next to it.

For example, you would see the same list with these additions:

- Wake up =
- Turn off alarm =
- Check notification on phone -
- Go to the bathroom =
- Take a shower +
- Get dressed =
- Make breakfast +
- Leave for work =

For someone who is learning to code, watching YouTube videos of non-programming topics might be a bad habit. Whereas someone reading a technical book for 30 minutes a night might be a good habit.

If you have any difficulties with scoring each of your habits today, ask yourself the question "Does this behavior help me become the type of person I wish to be?"
The process of changing your behavior always starts with awareness, and creating a scorecard will help you acknowledge your current equilibrium.

When and Where
The cues that can trigger a habit can come in a wide variety of forms. Whether that's starting your favorite music playlist, looking at the clock, or the sound of your alarm.

Generally speaking, to implement a habit you might follow the general format:

When X happens, I will do Y.

* * *

You do this today and you might not even notice it. You wake up in the morning and might take a shower directly after. Not only does this increase the odds you will perform the action, but being aware of it helps you understand how to improve it.

Without this basic detail, you may actually fall short in creating a system for the outcomes you want. For example, if you say "I'm going to read more technical books" or "I'm going to code more", we are really leaving it up to chance that we will actually remember to do it. This fades away with time if we do not create a backing system.

It's not always obvious when you should take action, and you might wait your entire life for the time to be right to make an improvement. Instead of waiting for the action, follow a predetermined plan instead.

A simple method to apply this is to fill out the following sentence:

I will [BEHAVIOR] at [TIME] in [LOCATION].
- Programming. I will code for 30 minutes at 7 pm in my room.
- Reading. I will read for 20 minutes at 8:30 am in my kitchen.
- etc

If you aren't sure of the [TIME] to start, make a commitment to start at the first of the week, first of the month, or even first of the year. There is no reason you cannot start by committing today and acting upon it tomorrow.

The more specific you are with your commitments, the more focused you are on completing the action. This details the how with regards to completing your habit.

Habit Stacking

When it comes to building new habits, you can connect behaviors with one-another to your advantage. One such way to build a new habit is to identify a habit you currently do each day and then stack another habit on-top of it. This is known as habit stacking. You can use habit stacking to plan your whole day if you'd like, however start small by using the following formula:

After [CURRENT HABIT], I will [NEW HABIT].

- Programming. After I pour a cup of coffee each morning, I will code for 30 minutes.
- Reading. After I eat dinner each evening, I will read for 20 minutes.
- etc

The key to being successful with your new desired behavior is to tie it alongside something you already do each day. This allows you to gain momentum by going from one habit to the next.

As I mentioned earlier, you can use this to plan your whole day. Here is an example of how your evening routine might look like:

1. After I get home from work, I will cook dinner for 30 minutes.
2. After I eat dinner, I will code for 30 minutes.
3. After I code for 30 minutes, I'll read a technical book for 20 minutes.

This process is really flexible as you can insert and remove any behaviors from your current routines. For example, if you wanted to read even more in a day, you might insert a habit to read for both your morning and evening routines. Take for example the following morning routine: Wake Up > Take a shower > Cook Breakfast.

Inserting a habit is as simple as putting it into before and after an existing habit:

Wake Up > Take a shower > Read for 20 minutes > Cook Breakfast.

* * *

It does not matter how you decide to use this strategy other than the fact that you are selecting the right cue to kick everything into gear. Know that there are right and wrong times to insert habits into your routine.

Use your existing habit scorecard to find the best places to insert a new habit into your lifestyle.

Designing Your Environment

Your environment is an invisible hand that shapes your behavior. Regardless of your unique personality, you will notice that your behavior depends on the environment you're in. If you're in a library, you might be quiet. If you're at a concert, you might be loud. Each of our habits depends on the context that backs it.

The more obvious and available something is, the more likely you will use it. It's not easy to practice programming if your computer is tucked away in a backpack. It's not easy to read technical books if your books are sitting on a bookshelf away from plain eyesight.
To battle this, you should design your environment to work for you, not against you.

- If you want to read every night, put your book on your counter.
- If you want to program every night, put your computer on your coffee table.
- etc

The more obvious the cue, the more likely you'll think about that habit throughout the day. You will increase your odds of fulfilling the habit simply by preparing your environment. This helps you make better decisions and will become natural when everything is right in front of you.

Habits can be easier to change in a new environment. By redesigning your environment, you can get a fresh start by removing negative associations with positive ones instead.

* * *

- Can't read at your apartment because of neighbors being loud? Go to a coffeeshop.
- Not being productive at work? Find a focus room.
- etc

Try to associate a single environment with an action you complete. For example, you might always study on your kitchen table and you might code in your bedroom. Try not to associate too many actions with a single environment as you may not be able to differentiate the actions throughout the day. For example, if you sit in your bedroom doing reading, coding, watching tv, playing video games, and more, it can be quite difficult to cue our habits.

Reducing Exposure

Self-control is difficult to manage as it's typically linked to our perseverance, grit, and willpower. You may wish you were a more disciplined person, but ultimately you can be one by creating a more disciplined environment.

Bad habits will find a way to feed themselves. You'll have a bad day and you'll realize that you just watched shroud on Twitch to numb the pain.

You can break a habit if you're aware of it, however it might be impossible to forget it. Restraining temptation is not an effective strategy because it takes up too much energy. Sure you can do this in the short run, but in the long run you won't be able to keep up.

Instead you need to cut off the bad habits at the source. You need to reduce exposure to the cue that causes it.

- If you can't get work on a side project done, you may need to block Twitch to prevent you from watching.
- If you're playing too many video games, put the console away in a hidden place every time you're done using it.
- etc

* * *

You may be surprised at how effective it is to simply remove the cue. You'll notice these behaviors to fade away with time.

Making Habits Attractive

Habits that are attractive are ones that appeal to you to actually do. You can make your habits more attractive by pairing your habits with wants and needs, finding a culture that wants the same things you do, getting into a kick-ass routine, and reframing your mindset.

Pairing Habits

Dopamine is released when you experience pleasure, but also when you anticipate it. Whenever you predict an opportunity will be rewarding, your dopamine will spike in anticipation. As your dopamine rises, so does your motivation to act.

For us to take action however, it is not the reward itself, but rather the anticipation of it. A reward system is a way you can anticipate this rush of dopamine as you keep wanting the reward.
Every action you take is because of the anticipation that comes before it.

To create a reward system, you can bundle temptation with your habits. For example, you might pair a habit of programming, with a reward of playing a video game after you finish. You can also bundle temptation at the same time.

You will find a habit attractive if you do one of your favorite things at the same time.
Use the following formula to bundle and stack your habits:

- After [CURRENT HABIT], I will [HABIT I NEED].
- After [HABIT I NEED], I will [HABIT I WANT].

For example, if your one thing you absolutely want is to play video games to unwind from work you might bundle and stack habits in this way:

* * *

- After I get home from work, I will code for 60 minutes (need).
- After I code for 60 minutes, I will play a game of Fortnite (want).

This will make you look forward to doing the things you need to do versus the things you want to do. You will associate a good relationship with these habits by bundling your wants and needs.

Culture Fit

You may not realize it, but our earliest habits are simply because we try to imitate those around us. We follow a script given by our friends and family members just to fit in. You may have heard the old saying that "An apple doesn't fall far from the tree", and you'd be right, because the habits you grew up with are instilled in your brain.

As we grow older, we start to adapt the habits of those close to us, the majority of people, and those we believe are powerful.

Being around people will shape your habits directly. Specifically the social environment you're involved in will give us cues to copy the way people handle certain things such as getting work done, relaxing after work, and more. You may imitate behavior more often than you think. The closer you get to someone or a group of people, the more you may adopt the norm from others.

One of the most effective things you can do to build better habits is to surround yourself or join a culture where your desired behaviors is the normal behavior.

Nothing will keep you motivated other than feeling like you belong among a group of people.

Whenever we are unsure on how to behave, we look to the majority of people to guide our behavior. You might ask yourself, what would everyone else be doing? What is everyone else thinking? What do people on Reddit/Facebook/Twitter have to say about how I should behave?

The problem with this is that you lose what makes you unique, your individuality. When you change your habits and that might mean challenging the social norm, you should know that it will feel difficult, even against the grain. But do know that it is perfectly okay to do your own thing.

Finally, we are drawn to behaviors of the highly effective people. For example, you might follow Dwayne "The Rock" Johnson on Instagram and start to adopt his habit of hitting the gym extremely early in the morning.

The reason we're drawn to these people is that we desire their success ourselves. Most of our habits are imitations of people we admire and we try to replicate them by seeing a recipe already written, to which we try to create. We want the high status feeling of approval, respect, and praise of others. If any behavior can get us those feelings, we will find that habit to be attractive.

We also are motivated to avoid any behaviors that would otherwise lower our status. Imagine how fast you are to act when you get word that your parents will be visiting from out of state next week and your house is a mess. Although this is a temporary way to alter your behavior, the underlying reason is we are worrying about what others might think of you.

Kick-Ass Routine

Each of your behaviors has a craving and motive. A craving typically takes form such as "I want to do something". However the underlying motivation that drives that behavior can be hidden. Why do you want to do that thing? Does it:

- Bring you happiness?
- Bring you status?
- Bring you acceptance?
- Bring you connection?
- etc

At a deeper level, our motivations are driven by our feelings and emotions.

* * *

- Connect with friends = playing video games.
- Achieve status from friends, family, and yourself = studying programming.
- etc

One might learn to connect with friends by playing video games, whereas another person might head out to the bar with friends instead. Once you associate a solution with the problem you need to solve, you keep coming back to it. It becomes a habit.

Every day you are making your best guess of how you should act based on what you know works in the past or how you predict something will work.

Our feelings and emotions tell us whether to hold steady in our current state or to make a change. They are the driving force telling us how we should act. Habits are attractive when we associate them with positive feelings.

Reframe Your Mindset
You can make any hard habit more attractive by associating a positive experience with it.

For example, you might have to do homework for your computer science degree. Many people might associate this with a negative experience such as the dread of staying up late and struggling to learn new material in a short period of time.

Instead, consider it with a flipped mindset. You get to learn something new by doing this homework. It's an opportunity to prove yourself to your professor and to yourself.

The hard part is that if we associate a negative connotation with tasks that actually benefit us. Use the benefit to motivate you instead.

You can also adopt a motivation ritual prior to taking on a hard task. This might take form in something that makes you extremely happy when you do it. This could be watching your favorite YouTuber's latest video, playing with your dog, and much more.

* * *

You can transform your difficult habits into attractive habits by reframing how you think about them. Bring positive associations into the habit to kick-off your routine.

😌Making Habits Easy

Habits that are easy are ones that don't take much effort to do. You can make your habits easier by reducing any friction of the habit, priming your environment prior, mastering the now, thinking in terms of two minutes, automating where it makes sense, increasing the friction of bad habits, and giving yourself less choice.

😌Reduce Friction

One of the most effective ways to reduce friction associated with your habits is to design your environment which makes cues more obvious. However you can also optimize your environment. What this means is that you can ensure you are provided absolutely everything you need in order to just do the habit and not worry about anything else.

Every time you have to deal with something else, your mind switches contexts. Each time you switch contexts, you lose sight of the reason you are doing the thing in the first place. I like to call this the "Why am I in the kitchen again?" moments. You purposely went into the kitchen for one reason, and you ended up forgetting exactly why you went in there in the first place.

Every point of friction we can remove from our environments will help us in the long term. Instead of having a smartphone next to you while you code, try leaving it in another room. Instead of having a YouTube video playing on your second monitor, try leaving it empty for assisting your task at hand.

You should take advantage of those things that reduce friction for you. Make your process simpler, not more complex. Try removing friction points to gain benefits in the long term. This is known by addition by subtraction. Create an environment in which doing the right thing is as easy as possible. The less friction we have associated with our good habits, the more likely we will act upon them. The opposite applies with bad habits to which we would want more friction.

* * *

Prime Your Environment

When you walk into a room, everything should be in it's right place. Organizing a room for it's intended purpose will make your actions easy.

There are many ways to prime your environment for it's next use. If you want to code in the evenings after you get home from work, you might place your laptop on a table, place some headphones next to it, and have drinks available throughout the night.

The key here is that you are priming your environment prior to even using it. The only thing you have to do in this case is sit in a chair, everything else has been taken care of for you.

Similarly, if you are late to get out the door for work, what if you tried to place your clothes for the next morning out on your dresser and instead of worrying about choosing what to wear, you simply take a shower and get going.

You can take it to extremes if you'd like such as completely eliminating choices from your life. This is a common technique that people like Mark Zuckerberg or Steve Jobs, to which they wore the same outfit everyday to eliminate decision fatigue.

If you have any trouble with priming your environment today, ask yourself the following question: "How can I design a world where it's easy to do what's right?".

Mastering The Now

Have you ever had a day where it took one decision that you made which set the tone for the rest of it? You end the day thinking...If only I had done the other thing, my day would have felt more productive!

There's quite a bit of truth to that. Each of your choices is an entry point to a path of choices through your day.

* * *

This is why it's so important to stack good habits on-top of each other. The moment you decide between learning a new programming language and launching World of Warcraft, you are setting a fork in the road for future you.

As you may imagine, good choices lead to more good choices, and bad choices lead to more bad choices.

You start with launching World of Warcraft, after you're done, you decide to go get fast food, soon enough you are watching your favorite streamer on Twitch until it's time for bed. What happened to your goal of learning a new programming language?

We are limited by where each habit leads us. Being able to master the decisive moments throughout your day will set the direction for how you'll spend your time.

Two Minutes Or Less

When you start a new habit, you need to start small. By small, you need to start with the absolute minimal amount to get started.

Instead of letting excitement get the best of you, excitement is not sustainable for the long term.
Starting a new habit should take less than two minutes to do to start.

- "Learn a new programming language" becomes "Write one line of code."
- "Read thirty minutes of a Data Structure book" becomes "Read one page."
- "Work on a side project" becomes "Create a new project in your IDE."

By making your habits as easy as possible, there is very little resistance from just doing the thing. You can always start out small, and scale up later. Here's how you might scale with a side project.

* * *

- Very Easy - Creating a new project in your IDE.
- Easy - Write 10 lines of code.
- Moderate - Write 1000 lines of code.
- Hard - Write 5000 lines of code.
- Very Hard - Build a Side Project.

The actual work does not matter here. Rather getting into the habit of showing up for the habit is the main point. You can't improve a habit until it's established, so we're starting with square one.

Once you reliably show up every time for the habit, you can start to take on a larger routine. You might go from 2 minutes to 10 minutes. Weeks later, you might go from 10 minutes to 30 minutes, and so on.

The secret to continuing your habits strong is to keep them below a point where it feels like work. If possible, try to end on a high note where you're comfortable with stopping.

Most importantly however, the two minute rule is primarily used to cast a vote for your newfound identity. If you show up every day of the week to do 2 minutes of coding, you are casting a vote for your identity as a software developer.

Automate Where It Makes Sense

You can automate your habits by having a commitment device which is something that you use to lock in your future behavior. One such commitment device might be a commitment you have with another person. For example, say you were building a mobile application with a friend, and that friend has told you they are available to work on it every Wednesday at 7pm. This is a commitment device as it binds you to working on a mobile application. However a commitment device doesn't have to be a person. It can also be a thing, time, place, low-tech, or high-tech solution.

There are many ways to automate good habits while eliminating bad habits in the process. Typically this involves technology as it can take difficult behaviors into easy ones. However you can start today with a onetime action that will lock in good habits.

* * *

- Productivity: Social media, YouTube, Twitch browsing can be blocked with a website blocker.
- Distractions: Video games can be uninstalled off your phone and computer.
- Health: Help your back by buying a supportive chair.

The problem with onetime actions is remembering them at a later time. What happens if you install a new video game or find a new website that you replaced your previous habits with?

When you figure out ways to automate aspects of your life, you can spend your effort on the tasks that cannot be automated. This however is a double-edged sword as having the ability to automate things in our lives also provides us more free time to spend for our choosing.

Restraint is especially difficult given that you can virtually have anything you want in a matter of a few taps on a iPhone. You may notice that how you spend your downtime or breaks may turn out to be a bigger issue in itself. For example, imagine you took a YouTube break every 30 minutes of studying. Soon enough, you realize that you watched an hour and a half of YouTube and only studied for 30 minutes. These things can take over if we do not keep our eyes on them.

I use an app and website blocker everyday for a block of hours during the working days (9-5). I also use it to block out any downtime eaters in the times that I've dedicated to other things such as working on a side project, or live-streaming. This way, I have made it virtually impossible for me to waste my time, and ever time I try to waste my time, I'm reminded with a screen reminding me to realize my goals.

Increase Friction

With every step that you add to your bad habits, the more likely you will actually go through with them. By increasing the friction, you are more likely to just not find the habit attractive by the time you can actually get to it.

* * *

You can add more steps to your bad habits by first seeing how easy they are to do in the first place. For example, if you can't stop playing the latest God of War on your playstation, you need to add friction points to being able to play in the first place. You might:

- Complete various tasks before you can play.
- Retrieve the game console from a hidden place.
- Constrain your time you're allowed to play with a commitment device such as a timer.
- Only allow yourself to play when you're hanging out with somebody.
- etc

You can also associate playing the video game with an association of a good habit. For example, you might say for every 5 minutes of playtime, you must do an additional 5 minutes in the gym, or similar. The key is to find a commitment device that will work for you, and commit to it.

Paradox of Choice

The less choices you have, the more likely you'll be able to choose a good one. There are countless of things to distract you today, and they do a pretty good job of doing it. Whether it's selecting a new binge-watch on Netflix, who's live streaming tonight, or sinking time into a mobile game, we tend to let our old habits lead the way for how we spend our time. You can continuously restrict your choices by eliminating the choices that will not benefit you in the future.

Making Habits Satisfying

Habits that are satisfying are ones that make you feel great so you'll repeat them. You can make your habits more satisfying by treating yourself regularly, being aware of your bad habits, tracking your habits, avoid missing out twice, finding accountability partners, and using commitment devices.

Treat Yourself

You are more likely to repeat a behavior when you find it satisfying. Most of the time, you will experience the feeling of pleasure. Vice-versa, if you do not find a behavior satisfying, you are less likely to do it again. In short, what is rewarded is repeated. What is punished is avoided. Your good habits are associated with positive emotions, and can be destroyed with negative emotions.

The hard part regarding associating positive emotions is that we tend to find immediate satisfaction to be the important part. When we play video games, we get the immediate satisfaction of winning. When we go out to eat, we get the immediate satisfaction of taste. However when it comes to good habits, majority of the work is done for delayed gratification. In other words, you don't get the reward immediately.

- Bad Habits
- Immediate Outcome - Feels Good
- Overall Outcome - Feels Bad
- Good Habits
- Immediate Outcome - Feels Bad
- Overall Outcome - Feels Good

We now can say that what is immediately rewarded is repeated. What is immediately punished is avoided. Those who can delay their gratification in the long run will have outcomes than those who do not. If you delay playing video games and study a programming language, you'll generally know more at a job interview. If you delay watching Netflix and work on your side project, you'll ship to the app marketplace. Success in every field requires you to ignore an immediate reward in favor of a delayed one.

You can train yourself on delayed gratification by finding ways to provide an immediate reward associated with your good habits.

Awareness of Bad Habits

Good habits will feel worth it when they provide you with something tangible, whether that's more strength, more knowledge, or really any noticeable result. You've spent months learning a new skill, yet you don't see many results. You still have to google everything, you refer back to books or documentation all the time, and so on.

As you start out, you need a reason to stay on track and thus why immediate rewards are essential. While you're distracted with an immediate reward, the delayed rewards are working in the background.

As you use an immediate reward, this can be extremely helpful. However what about for things we want to stop doing such as playing to many video games or watching too much TV? It's quite hard to reward yourself for doing something you would typically reward yourself with.

What you can do is think of it in another way. For all the video games or TV you avoid, you reward yourself for not partaking. You might pay yourself the $60 on a new video game to go straight into a new computer, or you might spend that $10/month from Netflix on a couple cups of coffee. The immediate reward here is money towards other things, or even the time.

The key is to have an immediate reward that is not in the distant future. It should be obtainable to you within a year or so. Try not to conflict your reward with your good habits though. You wouldn't want to give yourself a Netflix binge watch for an hour if you are trying to manage your digital wellbeing.

✅Habit Tracking

The best way to measure your effectiveness of your habits is to track them. The idea for tracking your habits is very simple. You keep a record of all the behaviors you want to establish or abandon and during the day you mark which ones were successful.

This record can be as simple as a piece of paper on your desk, a habit journal, a wall calendar, or a mobile / desktop application. It doesn't matter which tool you use to track your habits. The important part is that you are tracking your habits.

By recording your habit, you are triggering a sense of completeness to which acts as a cue to start your next one. Habit tracking can provide you a sense of visual cues indicating how much progress you have made, this is heavily linked with how likely it will be with your success in long term endeavors.

* * *

Every time we track our habits, we are also being honest with ourselves. We are letting ourselves know whether or not we succeeded or failed with something we said we'd do. Instead of letting things slip day-by-day we are provided with a visible ledger showing the true reality.

The motivation you get from wanting to mark something complete each day can be empowering. As your streaks continue, so does your motivation to not break those streaks. You soon become the person who absolutely cannot miss a streak, and you get yourself in the mindset to continue the streak no matter what is thrown your way.

However habit trackers can also feel like they carry a burden. It's yet another thing to do every day, and you might be struggling with the habit itself. Tracking your habits is not for everyone, and you do not need to use it. You can use the power of automation to do this for you instead. If there is any measurement you can automate, it will save you time in the future. The only time you should care to manually track measurements is when they are the absolute most important to your goals.

Never Miss Twice

Life will get in the way of your habits, there is no denying it. Whenever this happens to you, you need to follow a simple rule. That rule is to never miss twice.

If you ever miss a single day of a habit, you absolutely need to get back into the fray as soon as possible. You'll break your streaks and you'll give in to temptation. One mistake will not ruin your progress, however two mistakes will.

Successful people have an ability that others do not possess; the ability to rebound from failure immediately. Be the person who shows up and proves that you have what it takes to work through bad days, sick days, impossible days even. Habits compound, and when you interrupt them, you lose progress faster than you gain it. Don't allow yourself to fall into an all-or-nothing mindset.

* * *

Accountability Partners

We hold ourselves accountable for every choice we make throughout the day. By the end of a day, we recall what we did that day and whether it was something we should have done or shouldn't have done. "Oh I really shouldn't have ate that much, or "I should've started my homework today".

However, there can be an easier way to take the burden off yourself everyday. Instead try to find an accountability partner. Ideally if you find someone who has the same goals and approach to obtaining those as you, it will make it much easier. However, really anybody who can hold you to your word will work. Not only will you keep each other motivated, but you will be on each other's conscious as you're acting on your habits.

There are a few things you should consider with regards to making an accountability partner work:

- Know exactly what you want out of an accountability partner.
- Make it a priority in your life.

- Give your accountability partner the benefit of the doubt. If they hold you accountable, it's no hard feelings.

Commitment Devices

Remember back when you were a kid and you would make promises to your parents or friends to do something? You promised to clean your room to go over to a friend's house. You promised you'd return that copy of Donkey Kong 64 after you were done playing it. This is also known as a habit contract.

Habit contracts are a very useful device to hold you to your commitments. They provide a penalty that are hidden to the naked eye. They provide a sense of humiliation and pain if they are not fulfilled.

For example, imagine you didn't clean your room to go over to a friend's house, not only are you letting yourself down, you also let your parents, and your friend down.

* * *

However, you're probably an adult by now and it's not something you think about day-to-day. You can however leverage a habit contract to benefit yourself and someone who holds you accountable.

Make it worthwhile for somebody to hold you accountable, give them something that would be very painful for you to lose if you fail. Whether that's $100, a prized item of value to you, or even offering to watch their pets.

You can use a habit contract against yourself so long as you hold yourself accountable. Want to learn a programming language in a month? Give yourself some criteria where you can hold yourself accountable. Don't let yourself watch TV for the next month if you fail, and raise the stakes if that doesn't get your attention.

Rise & Code

I was never a morning person. I found myself to be spending countless of hours at night hoping to be productive and get things done. However things were not getting done, and I would be groggy the following day.

⌛ Finding Your Schedule

I challenged myself to flip my schedule completely on it's head. I would embrace becoming a morning person for a little bit to see if I'm more effective or not. I would set my alarm for 6:00 AM and the first thing I did when I woke up was work on my business.

The night before, I would take a moment to write out exactly what I would do tomorrow in the morning. This helped my brain process the topic so once I awake in the morning, I'm freshly charged and already know how to make progress on the topic.

I found that I was much more productive first thing in the morning. I even went as far as logging my productivity at 6:00AM than my productivity at 8:00PM+. The results were obvious to me after a couple weeks, I was producing almost twice as much that I would have at night.

* * *

Why was I more productive first thing in the morning? For me it was the fact that I didn't have to go through other brain-intensive activities to finally be able to work on my own things. I didn't have to work for 8 hours that day, spend quality time with my family, take care of the house, etc. Instead I was able to provide my complete focus and precious time to be productive and efficient in the morning.

🛏 Optimal Rest

At a certain point you will need to stop working and set yourself up for success tomorrow. This requires you to go to bed earlier and eventually you'll develop a habit you'll adjust to.

You can use the time you prepare the night before to minimize your screen time, spending time with your family earlier, or get more time for yourself at night.

I do want to emphasize that you do not have to be an early-riser to make this work. The overall idea is to focus your energy and time by putting your most important task first in your schedule. This way there is no excuse that you didn't get around to practicing coding or working on a side project. Instead it's the first activity you engage in for your day to be productive.

▊Homework #5 - Get Into The Habit

By now you should understand the difference of systems and goals, how habits work, and how you can make your habits work for you and not against you. Now it's time to work on your habits to build routines & rituals that will help you learn more faster.

Here's what you should do:

- Go through your current habits by walking through your day in your head or as you do each habit and mark good habits with a (+), bad habits with a (-), and passive habits with a (=).
- For every bad or passive habit, ask yourself whether or not the habit will serve you in the future or not. If it will not, start to brainstorm good or other passive habits you can replace them with.
- Work to implement those habits in your routine by using I will <HABIT> at <TIME> in <LOCATION>.
- As those habits start to take form, start to stack your habits. After <Current Habit>, I will <New Habit>. Try your best to stack habits that are close in relation.
- Next, design your environment by looking at your good habits and finding ways that you can change up your environment to make it more likely that you'll do that habit such as tidying up your room, placing books in places you frequent, or setting your laptop on a table.
- When you start to complete the good habits that aren't easy to do nor fun to do, pair them with habits that are easy and fun to do. For example if you read 30 minutes of a JavaScript book, you can give yourself 30 minutes of playing a video game.
- Try to find a local or online group that is trying to do the same thing you're doing. If you're leaning how to code, go to a meetup about that technology or a user group. Maybe even try doing a hack-a-thon or game jam. Try to go to at least one a month if possible just to get a taste for it.
- Find ways to regularly make your habits easier. If you have any problem in doing them and have a way reduce

friction, do it! That can be as simple as buying a lamp because you don't have enough light at night to read, or buying a new computer because your code takes too long to compile on your ancient piece of tech.

• Work to prime your environment for your routine. This mostly means preparing your environment for the next time you use it such as charging your laptop, having a book opened to the page you left off, or even having snacks/drinks stocked.

• Last but not least, make sure that you are tracking your habits in some shape or form. If you miss a habit one time, that's okay. Just never miss twice. A calendar or journal is a great place to start and you can upgrade to technology or apps later.

Note: Habits are the bread and butter of what will make your learning successful. Take your time over the next few months just to build better habits for learning and continue to work on them your entire life.

CHAPTER SIX

Skills

* * *

SKILLS

Take any new skill head-on.

* * *

Active Learning

There are two main ways to learn a new skill quickly, actively & passively. With active learning, we are actively applying involved learning techniques to more effectively learn something new. With passive learning, we are not as involved. One good example is going to a lecture, some students just sit and listen to the lecture, that is best represented by passive learning. Some students on the other hand are listening, and actively taking notes or working with the material that is being presented. That is active learning.

3 The Three Main Techniques

There are three main techniques of active learning. Those are active recall, spaced repetition, and interleaving. Each of these techniques used alone can be extremely beneficial to learning new skills, but when you combine all three, you are able to accomplish things you never thought possible & your brain will thank you for it.

Active Recall

You may have at one point in your life struggled to re-read, highlight, or summarize what you just read. These aren't very effective ways of retaining information. A more effective approach is to use what is known as active recall. Active recall is pretty simple at it's core, you're simply retrieving information from memory on demand. There's a number of ways you can do this too, such as closing a book & trying to remember, covering an answer & guessing what it is, or even drawing your current understanding the best you can on paper directly from memory.

One effective method of active recall is using flashcards or a program called Anki to help you with active recall. The cool part about using software like Anki is that you can quickly put your question or definition on a notecard & it will even cover the next two sections through an algorithm as well.

Spaced Repetition

I used to be a chronic procrastinator. I would leave all of my studying to the last moment and cram as much as I could into my brain. There's another technique that is much more effective to help you retain information over a period of time, and that's spaced repetition. The concept is quite simple, you are going to repeat a certain type of practice in a spaced amount of time. The benefits are that if we spread out our reviews over time, we will remember things more effectively.

For example if you wanted to retain a bit of JavaScript knowledge you learned last week, you might want to revisit it this week or next week just to review that you still understand the main concepts or definitions. As hinted earlier, there are programs like Anki that can help you with spacing out your active recall, but it's always a good rule of thumb to revisit things we've already learned every so often just to ensure our understanding is still right.

Interleaving

The last method is to interleave the subjects or things you are learning so that you have a mixture of different things going on at one time. With programming, this should be fairly easy since you'll be learning about programming languages, frameworks, tools, and other things all at one time. Just know that interleaving is extremely beneficial and you should prioritize mixing what you're learning about as this helps you differentiate between different concepts and helps with memory associations. Once again, Anki can help you out here in which you can set an interleaving mode where you will be prompted different topics regularly.

A Little On Anki

Although Anki is one of the proven tools for doctors, lawyers, and other hard engineering, it is not necessarily the only way to actively learn. If you prefer to use these three techniques on your own, then the more power to you. It can be quite beneficial to build up your own Anki decks by creating questions on the things that challenge you throughout your learning journey. Additionally, you can probably find somebody else's Anki deck for computer science or various programming topics. Don't forget that sharing is caring & somebody else could likely benefit from you sharing your Anki decks publicly with them.

* * *

📖Chunking

Organizing what you're learning can be extremely beneficial. The idea of chunking mostly comes down to being able to break up something big into small logical chunks. These chunks are usually your overall understanding of something broken down into smaller chunks that you can easily digest.

💯Revisiting First Principles Thinking

At it's core, chunking builds on-top of the concept we learned earlier about first principles thinking. For a quick reminder, that is to break down the complexity into your most basic understanding by asking "Why" until you get there.

Chunking requires you to actively practice first principles thinking by breaking down complex and unwieldy topics into groups, patterns, or even for organizational purposes.

🎳Grouping

The first way to chunk is to group things to the point where they are easier to remember. There are many terms in software that are actually grouped things to help you remember easier. For example, the unix command "grep" is really just an acronym for "global regular expression print". As you may imagine, remembering the whole acronym is quite difficult, but knowing that "grep" prints based on a regular expression can help you group.

🧐Patterns

The second way to chunk is to find patterns in things so they're easier to predict & remember. If you noticed that most computing platforms use the number "8" to logically divide 8 bits into a single byte, or that every representation of memory is divisible by 8 (512 / 8), you may have noticed that this is a pattern that works because computers work in binary (base 2) and therefore is a good way to chunk information.

📚Organizing

The last way to chunk is to organize things based on their categorical meaning. This one is a bit more easy to understand as you're just placing things into areas that best represent your knowledge of them today. For example, for anything that might be in the category of "git commands" might be organized under a "version control" area in an organizer. Being able to break things into areas of understanding can help tremendously.

Quit While You're Ahead

Grinding through learning new skills or working on projects can burn you out quickly. It's simply not sustainable to spend long hours when you're only effective for so long every day. Instead of wasting your time, you should embrace the idea of quitting while you're ahead.

50% Rule

At least half of your time should be devoted to coding or building purely for its own sake. Not to learn, not to improve, not to develop your skills further, or even to apply what you've already learned. Rather, code and build the things that you're interested in. In other words, think of if you were the most talented programmer in the world today, what would you be coding right now? Spend 50% of your time doing just that.

Never Less Than, Never More Than

Setting expectations for yourself to quit is a good idea. You can embrace the idea of "never less than X, never more than Y". It's a simple way to set the bounds as to when you should call it quits. For example, you might read a coding book for never less than 15 minutes, never more than 90 minutes every day. What about coding though? You might code for never less than 30 minutes, never more than 120 minutes. Whatever the boundary is for you can really help you feel satisfied everyday when quitting.

Optimal Stopping

As you start to set expectations for yourself to quit, you're going to find an optimal stopping point. This is usually a specific amount of time that is "just right". Nobody will be able to tell you the exact optimal stopping point but you. Sure you can go read through the science on the topic, but really it comes down to what will be consistent for you everyday.

* * *

✓ Linear vs. Residual Results

There are certain skills that we will learn that produce very linear results. This might be a one-to-one ratio such as how much time you put into something might make you a certain amount of money. Don't forget that your brain is a residual machine, results will flow to you whether you put in the effort or not. These results will come to you when you're sleeping, exercising, or just relaxing. You can lose out on these residual results by trying to do something linear in it's place. Make room for your residual results by calling it quits.

✎ Daily, Weekly, Monthly, and Yearly Reflection

To stay current with your skill acquisition, you should be checking in with yourself as much as it makes sense for you personally. I recommend that you check in at least daily similar to the idea of daily standups, but also that you consider reflecting after each week & every month just to ensure you are able to see how far your goals have come since then.

Daily Reflection

As mentioned earlier in this book about daily standups, being able to plan & reflect upon each day is important in the learning process. You'll be able to write down what you want to get out of the day each morning, and then quickly write about what you accomplished that day in the evening. This can be a powerful exercise if you consistently do it as you'll always know what you're doing and whether or not it's working for you and the challenges each day may bring.

17 Weekly Reflection

Zooming out a little bit, you may want to consider a weekly reflection in which you go through each of your days and try to get an understanding if the week was an overall success. You might first go into the week by planning it with a few items you want to accomplish or get done, and then reflect upon how you did with each of those items. These items should be in the scope of lasting around a week, which should realistically be able to be completed in a couple days of work.

* * *

Monthly Reflection

Zooming out even further is the monthly reflection, and one of the more important reflections in my opinion. Sometimes life will pass by quite quickly and we'll see a month go by without even noticing. This is where we can account for both our daily reflections & our weekly reflections to see how well we performed compared to our expectations. Typically a month is a long enough period of time to accomplish a number of things such as picking up a new skill, and being able to get a good feeling of how far you are in that process is why the monthly reflection is my favorite.

Yearly Reflection

Last but not least is the yearly reflection. The yearly reflection can be both empowering & even disappointing. The yearly reflection is more of an exercise to set yourself up for the next year. It challenges you to really think in terms of what the big picture items were for your last year. What were your large accomplishments? What did you learn? What are you going to do better next year? Those types of things. I love doing yearly reflections because they help me understand how much I'm compounding year after year. Although your first couple might be a little disappointing, once you build the habits & ability to rapidly acquire skills, you'll be empowered every year after that.

Focused and Diffused Modes

There are two main modes of learning that you should know about while acquiring new skills quickly. These two modes will help you shift your focus & attention as it's needed and give you the peace of mind that procrastinating is actually productive. I mentioned this earlier in the "Fast Brain, Slow Mind" chapter, but we'll dive in a bit deeper so you know what to expect.

Focused Mode

Your focused mode is how you approach solving problems & is generally associated with how you concentrate on something. We only have a certain amount of attention and willpower to focus everyday. When that's all used up, we need to get into the habit of giving ourselves enough time to enter a diffused mode of thinking.

* * *

Think about how long you're usually able to focus uninterrupted on something, is that 30 minutes? 60 minutes? Maybe even longer up to 4 hours? Whatever it might be, know your limits & know when to call it quits so your brain can do all the heavy lifting.

Diffused Mode

Your diffused mode on the other hand is how you relax your attention & allow your subconscious to do majority of the work for you. Many programmers get into this mode when they are not actively working on something. This is the whole idea of solving problems in the shower. Your brain is doing the work behind the scenes without you even realizing it.

The challenge however is that many people don't know how to relax. They think that every hour spent outside of focusing is wasted or could be better spent on learning. This couldn't be further from the truth as being in a relaxed state is crucial to being able to learn quickly. So what do you do? You need a healthy balance of the two.

Balancing Act

As mentioned earlier, focused & diffused modes are really a balancing act and can vary per person. I'm the type of person who likes to have at least two deep work sessions everyday which span an 8 hour workday. I then have a single shallow work session which spans 4 hours that then leads into diffused time to do things I enjoy & have nothing to do with what I am working on. You can learn much more about my personal workflows in the workflows chapter, but just know that you will have to find what works out best for you.

Mental Models

If you can explain something complex to a 5-year old, you've truly mastered a skill. The quality of your thinking depends on the models that are in your head that you understand and can share with others. When you learn to see the world as it is and not as you want it to be, everything changes. The solution to problems becomes clearer and you can view them through perspectives you might not have prior.

* * *

Blind Spots

The programmer with the least amount of blind spots will win. This is a skill of finding the right solutions for the right problems. Come from another perspective, if you can avoid problems entirely, you have less blind spots. To have less overall blind spots, you can learn more about mental models to help shape your overall thinking.

How Something Works

A mental model is simply a way to describe the way something works in the world. They shape how we think, understanding, and form beliefs around something. It's how we spot patterns, create metaphors, and how we largely think and reason about them.

When you think of something like a computer, how exactly do you describe your representation of how it works to somebody else? It's hard right? We can't keep all these details in our brains, but we can give a close analogy as to what it closely resembles.

Mental Models Are Used Everywhere

Want to know something funny? You've been exposed to a number of different mental models so far in this book. I've talked to you about first principle thinking, Pareto principle, circle of competence, and Occam's razor to name a few. You probably didn't even know these have an official name as you related with them in some fashion already.

Let's take Occam's razor for example. The goal of this book is to help someone teach themselves a complicated skill like programming for someone to pickup in their part-time. This book tries to accomplish that by giving simple explanations for what is needed to be successful in learning a skill like programming. In short, rather than trying and wasting your time understanding things you don't know, you can build upon the things you do know today & branch out slowly.

JIT & AOT Learning

Not everything you learn will be used right away. This doesn't mean that it's not important to learn, but rather for you to understand that there are two different types of things you'll learn on your journey.

* * *

Just In Time (JIT) Learning

One of the most effective ways to learn something is to learn it just in time before we need to use it or even while we use it. This is the tried and true way of being "hands on" with our learning. If you can apply something directly, you can learn it quickly.

This can be beneficial to you. You don't need to know everything under the sun about compilers, build tools, or even web servers. You do need to know how to build a project and deploy it to a server though.

Throughout your learning you should try to make as much of your learning "hands on" or "just in time". The more familiar you become with doing something, the more likely you'll do it again & retain it.

Ahead of Time (AOT) Learning

On the other hand there is learning something for the sake of knowing or the potential of using it in the future. Depending on how you see it, this can largely be a bet of whether it will pay off for the time spent. This to me is what I call "ahead of time" learning. In most cases, this type of learning is used at some point in your career. For example, I cannot count the times where my basic knowledge of a compiler came to save the day. I spent maybe a few hours just to understand the mental models of a compiler & it helped save me many more hours in debugging.

Although this type of learning can pay off in the future, it largely depends on what your goals are. If you're never going to be interested in data analysis, then all the time you're staring at documentation for pandas will not serve you today. Try to keep in mind that although you might be learning something for it's future potential, that you make a priority to learn the things that will get you one step closer towards your goal each day.

80/20 Learning

Try to make 80% of your learning oriented towards just in time learning. Follow your natural curiosity and learn things on the spot. This can be as simple as following google searches for common things you want to do like "how to build a website", "for loop in C#", or "write a compiler".

The other 20% of your learning should be learning things you may not necessarily use in the near future, but rather about subjects you're interested about or that you want to become more knowledgeable about in the future. This can be topics like advanced Linux operators, microservices, or even docker.

Learning Styles

Everyone has their own learning style that they prefer. For some that might be visuals, for others that may even be listening. There are many learning styles & combination of learning styles that you'll have to explore to find the one that fits you best.

Visual

A visual learner learns best through written language and visuals. For programmers, that might be reading books, reading documentation, following tutorials, and so on. If there is something that can be shown to a visual learner, that is where they thrive.

Auditory

An auditory learner often listens deeply and asks questions as they come up. For programmers, that might be asking questions, posting on mailing lists/forums, and so on. If there is something that can be talked about to an auditory learner, that is where they'll shine.

Kinesthetic

A kinesthetic learner is hands-on and needs to experiment. For programmers, that might be testing new commands, running code to see if it fails, and building programs. If there is something that can be shown or built by a kinesthetic learner, that is where they'll excel.

Combined Learning Styles

If we're being realistic, no single learning style is more effective than the others. In most cases, you're going to be combining the learning styles based on your personal preferences. For me, I fall quite neutral under an even split of each of these learning styles. When I first started my programming journey, I was more of a visual learner and as time grew on, I became a more auditory learner. Now that I'm a bit further into my career, I have found myself mostly shifting towards kinesthetic.

The point is, don't worry too much about your learning style preference. Try to mix it up and combine the learning styles to become well rounded. Read books, follow tutorials. Ask questions, and get involved in communities. Try new things, and build cool shit.

Deliberate Practice

Deliberate practice is a special type of practice that is purposeful and systematic. Regular practice might represent repetition, **deliberate practice requires focused attention with a goal of improving.**

Getting Into Flow

Deliberate practice will keep you in a state of flow, where your work will be hard enough to make you uncomfortable and forces you to adapt.

One of the biggest challenges of deliberate practice is **staying focused.** Showing up and putting in your reps is the most important thing you can do. However, to take it to the next level, we need to break it down further.

The Pattern To Know

Deliberate practice follows this pattern: break down the overall process into smaller parts, identify your weaknesses, and try new strategies to improve overall. Rinse and repeat.

Say for example, you are struggling with Data Structures & Algorithms. How can you break this down into smaller parts and identify your weaknesses?

Data Structures & Algorithms
- Big-O Notation
- Recursion

Sorting
- Insertion Sort

- Merge Sort 👍
- Quick Sort 👎

Data Structures

- Stack 👍
- Queue 👍
- Linked List 👎

Algorithms

- Depth First Search 👍
- Dijkstra's Algorithm 👎

Now you need to come up with a strategy to improve the 👎 items. Does it require more in-depth practice? Do you need to understand the concept from another lens? How can you then measure you improved?

Specific Feedback

A major difference between regular practice and deliberate practice is the way you get feedback to then improve upon. There are two ways to get feedback:

- **Measurement** ✏️ - You keep data to understand your baseline, your delta, etc
- **Coaching** 🏃 - Someone who finds small ways to help you improve, holds you accountable, etc.

You of course can use both methods to accelerate your deliberate practice. Deliberate practice is very meticulous. It's not only hard on yourself, but it's hard to do in general. If you're able to master deliberate practice, you can apply this to anything you want to become better at. You'll take an approach to explore, experiment, and refine your weaknesses until you have mastered them. At the end of the day, you'll have developed habits on your road to mastery.

Homework #6 - Learn How To Learn

By now you should have a good understanding of how you can quickly acquire new skills by using active learning techniques, quitting while you're ahead, reflecting regularly on your progress, using mental models to explain complex concepts, and using deliberate practice to achieve mastery.

Here's what you should do:

- When you're focused on learning, employ active learning techniques to help you retain more faster such as active recall (testing yourself), spaced repetition(repeating over time), and interleaving(mixing multiple subjects).
- Time box how long you'll focus and how long you can relax and rest for. A ratio of 8 hours focused(usually two 4-hour blocks) and 4 hours diffused is a good place to start and you can adjust as needed. Do know that these time blocks include regular breaks for eating, exercise, and more.
- Start to reflect upon each day, week, and month. Buy a journal or set a reminder to make sure you do it!
- Get a good understanding of your preferred learning style & start to cater your learning towards it.
- Employ some form of deliberate practice to get better at the things you aren't so great at. Use measurements or coaching to help you get better every day.

CHAPTER SEVEN

Job

* * *

JOB

Land the job by being yourself.

* * *

Kick-Ass Resumes

There's not much to having a stellar resume other than to keeping it as simple as possible. Not many people take this advice to heart and will try to make their resume stick out from the crowd or be accepted by an applicant tracking system(ATS) reader. These are not great ways to make killer resumes, but rather you should follow a few rules of thumb instead.

3 The Big Three

There are three main ingredients to a great resume. Those three are the following:

- Keeping it short & simple.
- Using language that your future role uses.
- Being as specific as possible.

Now you are on the path to a kick-ass resume, but let's also dive into some other things you should consider while we're at it.

15 Seconds Rule

Why do we follow those three rules above? Well, there's a high chance that when your resume gets into an actual human's hands, they will only spend about 15 seconds to read it. Think to yourself for a second, how much can you actually read in 15 seconds? I know personally, this is maybe one and a half glances at a piece of paper and being able to read the top half of a one-page resume.

Answer the Question

The main question you are trying to answer with your resume is the "why should we hire this person?" question. You're not going to check every box for a job's requirements, and in most cases you will be growing into a role, not having an impact from your first day. With this in mind, how can you show on your resume that you're either

1. The hardest worker in the room.
2. The right person for the job.
3. The best overall addition for the team's culture.

* * *

Formatting

When it comes to formatting, you should keep in mind a few things:

- Single column, single page.
- Order sections by most impactful/impressive to least impactful/impressive.
- Use a single link provider to centralize everything on your resume like your email, project urls, and more.

Using Language

I mentioned earlier about being as specific as possible. I cannot express how important this is when building your resume. If you built software for users, spell it out for those reading, what type of software? What did the software do? Who were the users? How many were there?

When you are being specific, use words that your future role or current role uses. Developers often use language around software development. These can be words like:

- Developed
- Built
- Implemented
- Engineered
- Documented (Maybe not this one since we know developers don't write documentation)

Talking About Experience

When you're talking about your experience & achievements, you can use a simple formula that will help you with all the rules we talked about above.

That formula is **[Accomplishment + Impact + Challenge]**

Here's an example of this in action.

- Developed a modern payment gateway using Authorize.NET for 50,000 hotel chains across North America improving average payment processing speed by 70%.

- Automated a CI/CD pipeline using GitHub Actions to ship production code to 150 e-commerce stores every week instead of once a month.
- Refactored and relocated server providers from Verizon to Azure which reduced operating costs by 90% and increased yearly uptime from 98%(7 days per year) to 99.5%(2 days per year).

💯 Optimal Stopping For Applying

There is a concept known as optimal stopping in which helps answer when you should optimally stop applying for a job. The magic number is 37% or 37. If you had a whole month to apply for developer jobs, you should stop applying after 37% or the first 11 days. If you do not get any offers after this, you should experiment with your application strategy and rework your resume.

If you're curious as to why, it can be simplified as to $1/e$ (which simplifies to 37%). Not every scenario will conform to this math theory, but it's worked well for me and it helps you know when you should stop trying with the same approach and take on a new one.

🆎 A/B Testing Your Resume

As mentioned earlier with the optimal stopping number after 11 days or 37 or so applications, you should also continuously experiment with your resume while doing this. Although you could send the same resume to companies you're interested in for 11 days or 37 applications, your odds are actually higher if you constantly experiment with your application each time. Try a new cover letter one time, change around your resume the next time, remove things that don't feel strong, reinforce things that are strong, and most importantly just have fun in the process.

🐱 Personal Portfolios

A personal portfolio can help you stand out from the crowd. If anything, it's your unique chance to make a great first impression without even knowing if people are viewing it. Your personal portfolio should be personal first and foremost. It should help somebody get to know you and who you are as an individual.

* * *

Personal Websites

For a programmer, your personal portfolio is usually some type of static site or blogging platform. If you are more oriented towards web development, you might even build your personal website yourself using your favorite technologies. Do know however that although this is an impressive thing to do, you don't need to do it. Rather it's more important to have a place on the internet where you can point people towards as your own personal brand.

Domain Names

For your domain name, it really doesn't matter. Use a name that uniquely is your own. That could be an avatar name you go by, your name, or a brand you're building on the side. Try to use a name that people can relate to. For example, don't use the names "simbs" or "skatez" because you used them in a past life when playing World of Warcraft (true story). Rather go with something that can uniquely identify you. I personally prefer using my full name because it's the easiest one that people can put a name to a face. I also use abbreviations of my name, but keep an artifact of my name somewhere in anything I host.

For actual domains, one cool thing you can do today is get a .dev domain. These domains have an intended use for software developers. When starting out, it's just important to grab a domain and you can figure more out later.

What Should Be On A Portfolio?

There's really no standard for what should be on a personal portfolio. Many people think that they need a flashy landing page or a whole navigation tree that dives into different aspects of you, but ultimately I find that your personal portfolio should best represent yourself while also giving more information to the reader.

What I think is important on a personal portfolio is the following:

- A little about you. Who you are, what you like to do, that type of thing.
- What your passion is & what your dreams are.
- A few projects that help show your passion & dreams.

- A bit about how you think by reading through your thoughts or blogs.
- Things you find cool in the world and want to share with others.

There's going to be people who tell you that your personal portfolio is your only opportunity to show your potential as a web developer, and that can be quite far from the truth. You have many more avenues to show your work that we'll dive into.

Grasping GitHub

There's one thing you can't really escape as a programmer, and that thing is GitHub. Most of the world's code is hosted on GitHub and contributions to software that powers the world is made on a daily basis there. Your GitHub profile & activity can help tell people who you are, what you work on, and the sort of projects you're interested in.

Open source is eating the world, and now is a good time to get involved based on your personal philosophy of it.

Why Does It Matter

As you start to contribute to the living system known as open source, you're putting yourself out there on the map. By simply being part of open source, you're opening yourself up to the various opportunities that can come with it.

For me, I got involved in open source and eventually was offered a job maintaining the very projects I was interested in. I got paid to do the very thing I escaped my day job to do. But jobs aren't the only opportunities that come from open source.

Many people have found success in various ways with open source. Some sell support to their OSS projects, some ask for donations to maintain a project they built from scratch, others build companies out of open source projects. The point is, opportunities are endless with open source.

Now you're able to work with like-minded individuals across the globe on common goals. It's easier than ever to find those people &

build cool things with them.

Repositories and Gists

There are two main artifacts that you create on GitHub, those are repositories of code and gists which are kinda like snippets. Of course each of these have a private and public mode to which you can choose whether or not you'd like to share them with the world.

For the things you want to share with the world, you want to make it as clear to the person stumbling across it what the thing is, how to use the thing, and how they might contribute to make the thing better.

Given you'll be working on many different projects in your lifetime as a developer, you should get into the habit of sharing code that you're going to abandon or throw away anyway. There have been so many times where someone has thanked me for sharing something that I planned to keep on a local hard drive forever. I've also expressed my gratitude to those who shared something they planned to throw out. As they say, one person's trash is another's treasure.

Contributions

There is another type of artifact that you create on GitHub, but others won't be able to necessarily see them. These are contributions to other repositories or gists. This is where I believe opportunities come from as you are actively going out to another repository and contributing in a positive way towards it.

Maintainers of these repositories will notice it, and those who repeat contributions tend to be the first in mind when those maintainers have special projects or are looking to hire more staff to help maintain it.

The most people will be able to see about your contributions is various shades of green bathroom tiles on your GitHub profile as a graph. Very rarely will someone look at your actual contributions unless they are really interested in your work.

GitHub READMEs

Within the last year or so, GitHub now allows you to create a profile README which is a special repository you create with your GitHub username and put a README.md file with markdown to help others who come across your profile get to know you a bit more. Previously you had a twitter-bio section worth of words that you can say who you are, but now you have endless opportunities to share a whole README worth of content to those who come across your profile.

Pinning What Matters

Just like your personal portfolio, GitHub allows you to customize pins of the repositories and gists that you are proud of and want to share with the world. The easiest rule of thumb to follow with regards to pinning is largely dependent on how much traction or showcase worthy the thing is. If you have impressive projects, pin them! If you have projects other people have starred, pin those! If you are building from scratch, pin the things that you best represents your skillset & future ambitions.

Being LinkedIn

There used to be a weird stigma about software engineers on LinkedIn. It is like that meme that goes around where theres a picture of a man clean shaven and another of the same man with a beard. The caption reads "unemployed programmer" and "employed programmer" respectfully. LinkedIn is very similar in my eyes, those who aren't employed are usually on it whereas those who are employed don't typically bother with it. LinkedIn however has become a professional social networking site where you can build a following and grow your opportunities as an individual. This has become even more mainstream in the last couple years alone.

The Basics

As someone who might be looking for a job, LinkedIn is your new online resume. It should largely be updated to reflect your resume and follow all of the tips we talked about earlier. The one thing you do get with LinkedIn that you don't with a resume is the opportunity to tell more about yourself. This can include a business-casual professional headshot, your location or geological areas you're interested in working at, a larger section to tell people about yourself, and a way to feature artifacts you created on the internet as a small portfolio of sorts. LinkedIn will guide you through all the basics, but I'll help guide you through some of the advanced tactics that may help you further.

* * *

Skills

LinkedIn uses a tagging system of various skills. These are skills that you can list and also be endorsed by others on your expertise or usage of them. They also serve as a way for recruiters can do advanced searches using LinkedIn recruiter tools. For jobs or areas of work you're interested in, it's a good idea to list the common skills In that area. It's not a great idea to keep a list of skills that you are no longer interested in working with or developing further.

There will be universal skills like the soft skills you build in the professional environment, but what I'm referring to is the technology skills you possess. For example, when I was early in my career, "jQuery" was the hottest thing since sliced bread. About 10 years after the fact, it's not a great skill to flaunt given the popularity of other frameworks like React and Vue. It's also not very likely that I'll find a job doing "jQuery" anytime soon either!

Premium

LinkedIn has a premium service that can be largely beneficial for you if you choose to use it. One of the biggest benefits you have as a job-hunter is that you can find recruiters for the companies that you are interested in working for. If you wanted to work for Roblox in California, you can easily search for people working on Roblox in California & reach out to their recruiter or hiring managers directly.

You can also save queries that will send you alerts when something new comes in. For example, if you were looking for a job using a specific skill or technology in your area, you can setup an alert for any activity in that area to be the first to know. These are usually job openings and similar that will help you apply & get your application on the stack.

On-top of the things you can do with it, there are some other techniques that I won't go into in this book, but do know that you can also send mails directly to people if you really want to get someone's attention and you believe your skillset is the right fit.

* * *

Sharing Your Job Hunt Story

The new normal on LinkedIn is motivational content about facing adversity & coming out the other end with a prestigious job. Don't let this distract you too much about what other people are accomplishing, but rather let it be an eye-opener that you can be doing the same thing. In my experience, finding a job in software engineering has been a shoe-in because the skill is in large demand, and companies are willing to take on just about anyone who is willing to learn on the job given how fast the industry moves.

Sharing your job hunt story definitely has more benefits than it does cons. You'll be putting yourself out there and sharing your progress towards landing a job, but on the other hand you might be putting a target on yourself with regards to how much a company can actually get you for. It all depends on your circumstances, but do know that you can share without having to share too many details that will do that to you. Social media can look like photoshop much of the time, so take this with a grain of salt.

Share the trials, the failures, the successes, and most importantly be like Kendrick Lamar and sit down, be humble.

Cover Letters That Stand Out

Your cover letters give you an opportunity to tell a story. A story about how the opportunity will give you an opportunity to grow and change as an individual. Don't sell yourself short. Everyone has a story worth sharing and your cover letter is your opportunity to do so.

Don't Copy

Cover letters are only unique because they come from the heart. Using a template or copying someone else's cover letter can come off in-genuine and awkward. I have only provided cover letters that came straight from how I felt about the opportunity. They were not about putting the company or opportunity on a pedestal. Rather it was my perspective about what the opportunity meant towards the growth & change of me individually. Would I have opportunity to grow in this role? How would landing this role change me for the better? Those things are infinitely more interesting than a mad-libbed cover letter template.

* * *

🏰Storyworthy

The best cover letters tell a story. That story has a 5-second moment that will culminate realization and transformation. Think to yourself about your story for a second. When was the last time you realized that you did something challenging, scary, or even risky and it changed your perspective forever? You'll probably have a few of them.

Here's a few of mine:

- Got my first website programming job in high school with zero experience. This made me feel like someone is willing to take a chance on me.
- Graduated with a CS degree & passed hard math/computer theory classes. This made me feel empowered that hard-work pays off.
- Landed a job at a startup & was eventually acquired by Microsoft. This made me feel like anything is possible.
- Started making content for software developers and putting myself out there to be judged by the world. This made me feel passionate to share with others.

Each of these moments changed my perspective. The first job led to a degree, the degree led to a startup job, and that startup job led to me wanting to help other people become software engineers.

Now that you've found your 5-second moment, you can work to find a beginning and an ending. You probably think this is hard to do, but try to not take it too literally. The beginning should be a place that feels right to begin. You don't start a story at the birth of the main character, rather you start it right before the main character meets their first challenge (also known as your 5-second moment). As for your ending, you want to put on your thinking hat and visualize how you imagine your future to be for the opportunity or what you want out of it. Imagine yourself in a year into it, what would you have wanted to accomplish by then? That's your ending.

💼Prepping for Interviews

Interview preparation can be quite stressful and tough. The

unfortunate reality of the current industry is that your preparation for interviews is largely a one time thing. Once you've got your foot in the door, you really don't have to go through an obnoxious vetting process including theoretical scenarios, whiteboards, and a whole lot of condescension.

Matching your experience

Be prepared to talk about everything you put down on your resume. You're going to be asked about your experience and projects that you were involved with. They'll ask you what technologies you used, the challenges you faced, and even about how you might approach a problem they have that is similar to something you previously did.

The reality of LeetCode & data structures / algorithms

In most technical roles, you're going to have technical questions to assess your understanding. In my opinion, many of these are not very practical to what you're actually going to be doing on the job, but that's beside the point.

The reality we live in today is that many employers will use LeetCode & data structures / algorithms as a means to weed out candidates. Practicing these types of questions and understanding the inner workings of them can be very useful to your success in interviews.
Most companies (even big tech) will use easy-medium level questions to assess the understanding of an applicant.

Of course you'll be asked different things depending on the role you're applying for, but the foundations of CS, big O notation, sorting algorithms, and much more are going to be fair game. If you're lucky by the time you read through this book, the industry will have moved on to more practical challenges that relate closer to the on-job duties rather than what you might encounter in a ACM coding championship.

Know your why

Similarly mentioned in the previous section about cover letters, you should really get to understand your "why" with regards to why you want to take on the opportunity. Take some time to really get to know the company, understand their business, and future opportunities they're taking on. The more you know about the company, the more impressive you'll look when it comes to interview time.

☕Rest up because you'll need it

Last but not least, make sure that you get enough rest. Don't show up to an interview looking like a zombie who spent hours cramming or needlessly preparing. There's not much of a benefit to stress over a single interview. Get your mind off of everything the day beforehand & when you show up, don't be afraid to be authentically you.

🎙 Interviewing Like a Pro

There's one secret to interviewing like a pro, and that's simply being yourself. It's easier said than done, but we'll cover the different things that will help you interview like a pro. I'll tell you what has worked well for me, and give you a perspective as to what might make you stand out.

👔Dressing the part

There's one simple rule you should keep in mind when it comes to interview attire. That rule is this. Dress one notch higher than the normal. If the office mostly dresses casual, then you dress business-casual. If the office dresses business-casual, then go rent a suit if you must. The reality is that most developers will fall into the casual to business casual range depending on where they work. A one time event where you dress fancier is not going to kill you, but will leave a lasting impression.

🤷 Don't be afraid of "I don't know"

There's often a trap in which you're asked a question and you think that you're expected to know the answer. Here's a trick, when you don't know something, you simply say "I don't know, but I'd love to know the answer". You're not going to know the answer to every question, that's just the reality of it all. If you get stuck at anytime or do not have a good answer, your best answer is "I don't know" and to move forward. The worst you can do here is try to bluff your way through it.

* * *

The power of "Yes, And"

When you're talking to the various people who will be interviewing you, follow a simple rule. Whatever you might be talking about, use a concept of "Yes, And". What this means is that you accept the reality presented to you, and you add upon it. This makes you much more interesting as you are building possibilities rather than just answering questions. Think about it this way, instead of just answering a question with a yes or no, you are answering a question with a yes, and which leads to much more interesting conversations.

Assessing Your Interviewer and Company

Job interviews can have some of the strangest power dynamics of any conversations you may have. It's common to feel like your interviewer holds all the power and you are simply there to wait for their judgement call. Sure your interviewer is assessing you, but that's the point of the interview. The conversation should however not be a one-way street. You should also be assessing your interviewer, the job, and the company right back. You are there to figure out if you're the best match for the job and you're there to figure out if it's the best match for you.

Be Yourself

If it can be stressed any further, it is to just be yourself. What I mean by this is that you aren't afraid to act as if you would 5 years into the job. You need to bring your authentic self to the interview because your authentic self is how you show that you're going to make an impact for years to come at the company. Don't put up a barrier on act differently than you would at home or in front of friends, rather you should embrace that side of you because it's infinitely more interesting than a serious version of yourself and will make you more personable.

Homework #7 - Job Preparation

By now you should have a good understanding of what makes a great resume, how to build a portfolio on various platforms, writing cover letters that stand out, preparing for interviews, and how to interview like a pro.

Here's what you should do:

* * *

• Get your resume into shape and experiment with sending out different versions of your resume and cover letters when applying to jobs.

• Update your portfolio, GitHub, LinkedIn, and other platforms to help tell your developer story so far.

• Know your optimal stopping point for applying for jobs using the same resume & cover letter. Try for the number 37 and track this so you know when you should change things up.

• Treat your job hunt as a funnel. # of applications > # of phone screens > # of interviews > # of offers. Use this as data to help you and track it!

• When interviewing try to relax as much as possible and just be yourself. The easier you make it on yourself, the easier it will be to perform.

CHAPTER EIGHT
Building

* * *

BUILDING

Build in the open and show the world.

* * *

Building In Public

One easy way to be recognized for the things you're doing anyway is to build in the public. Building in the public is a fancy way of saying "sharing with the world". As you make progress on your projects, learn cool new things, and challenge yourself with interview preparation or complicated subjects, you should share your findings with the world.

Open Source

Publishing your work to an open source repository is one great way of sharing with the world. These repositories can be resources you've collected, projects you're working on, alterations to popular projects, and much more.

GitHub and other open source git providers are some of the biggest search engines in the world. That can mean that people stumble upon your work and may even follow you!
You can also contribute to other projects which will show that you're an active contributor in the open source community & others may see the type of contributions you're providing.

? Question Sites

Posting questions and answers can help build up your knowledge while also benefiting the world. You may encounter errors, issues, problems, and much more throughout your everyday programming and contributing to question sites such as Stack Overflow can be very beneficial in the long term.

By taking a few minutes out of your time to help improve an existing question, ask a question of your own, provide a more accurate answer, you name it, it will benefit everyone involved and chances are you may even run into that issue in the near future.
Although majority of people just read other people's answers, you can really make a name for yourself by helping others with the things you're running into on the way.

* * *

Blogs

As a means to share whatever is on your mind, you can use a blog to talk about things you learned, things that are cool to you, tutorials for others, and much more. There's no one-sized fits all blog out there, and you can even just blog about specific tech if you wanted as well! Blogs are great because you own them at the end of the day. That means that you have ultimate freedom of what you put on them & how others interact with them.

Having a personal blog is one of the most important things you can have as a developer. Many developers actually don't have a blog or personal website, and this helps show to others how you think through problems and how you communicate with others.

Social Media

Social media is a fickle beast because it means putting yourself out there for others to judge. Some of the best ways that you can leverage social media is simply by sharing your journey with the world. That last sentence may scare you initially, but let's talk about it. Many developers live second lives on twitter, some on YouTube, and some even on Twitch. Different social medias serve different purposes for how you prefer to share with the world. If you like to share bite-sized snippets or funny memes about programming, twitter or reddit might be your go-to.

If you like to share tutorials or articles, then YouTube or dev.to might be best. If you like to just hang out and try new things and learn with others, then Twitch or TikTok might be your thing. Whatever it is, try to get comfortable with being uncomfortable by putting yourself out there on social media. The only rule for social media is that you should be providing value to someone on the other side of the screen. I'll let you figure out what that value means in the meantime.

Videos

Videos are the new gold when it comes to tech content. Previously it was books, blogs, and manuals. Now it's visualized content that can be found on YouTube, Twitch, and TikTok type platforms. Videos can be anywhere from 15 seconds long(TikTok) to hours long (YouTube). Some videos can be as simple as showing off your favorite IDE shortcut, or going over your top 10 favorite VS Code extensions. Whatever it might be, videos can help others because they are easily consumed. Your 60-second video on the top programming languages might even inspire thousands of people to learn to code. There's a virality to videos that makes this type of building in public my favorite personally.

Live Streams

Live streams for coding are on the verge of being some of the best content out there. There's not much pressure to be perfect on a live stream, and also there's tons of room for mistakes to happen which makes them human. Programming live streams can be done really well with high production for a specific tutorial, but they can also be a person sitting in their room with a webcam running into syntax errors all night.

The one piece of advice I would give you regarding live streaming programming is that programming is in itself a very boring thing to watch. Rather than an emphasis on the programming part, think about how you can provide more entertainment for others outside of the topic of programming!

Package Managers

Many programming ecosystems have a concept known as a package manager. A package manager is a centralized feed of libraries that authors have published and can be used by anyone in the world with an internet connection.

If you create a cool library, template, or even a tool that another person can leverage, you should consider publishing it to the package ecosystem that you're involved with. People will try it out, give you feedback on your GitHub and help you improve it over time.

Contributing To Open Source

With over 56 million developers using platforms like GitHub and over 1.9 billion contributions every year, open source continues to grow at an absolutely insane pace. Open source is just code that is publicly accessible, distributable, and most importantly, provides a way for you to contribute directly to it.

* * *

Building Your Skills

One of the best reasons to get into open source software is to extend
your current skillset towards one that is more open in nature. This is in
my opinion the most practical type of skills you can develop that will
mimic the real workplace. You'll be working with other people on the
internet to review contributions, merge code into the project, and
prepare releases for public consumption.

Trust me when I say that anybody can contribute to open source. When
I was early in my career, I could barely write code, so I found ways to
contribute to open source projects instead until I could. This was the
little things like writing documentation, creating samples, helping
close issues, and much more.

If contributing to other people's projects isn't too interesting to you,
you can always create your own projects & have other people
contribute to yours. Sharing with the world your ideas, software that
embody those ideas, and allowing others to build upon it is one of the
best ways to build mastery in software development.

Find Like Minded Individuals & Projects

Open source is huge. With over 60 million new repositories being
created in the last year alone, the chances to find like minded
individuals and projects are a sure thing. Depending on the
development ecosystem that you're most familiar with, you might
want to look to projects that you enjoy, you want to improve, and
you'll grow with.

Some of the most intelligent & caring individuals I've met in my life
have been through open source. Hell, I even got a job doing open
source & have been doing it for majority of my career. If you can find
these types of people & projects, you'll know that you're in good
company & can build a life off of it in my cases.

Build a Reputation

What exactly does it mean to build a reputation in open source? I'll
give you at least my perspective. That means being annoying enough
by providing valuable contributions to a project that the maintainers
start to take notice. As they see your valuable contributions increase,

they may even want to ask you to become a maintainer of the project in some way. Even if you aren't contributing code to a project, but do other reputation building type things like evangelizing the project, writing documentation for the project, or even helping with the project management side of things, you'll surely be able to start building a reputation.

You Don't Have To Contribute Code

Perhaps there is a stigma in open source that all contributions have to be ones with code. In fact, majority of commits to open source projects tend to be lower fidelity like fixing typos, changing version numbers, adding documentation, and much more.

If you are not in a position to contribute code as you're still learning the code base & working to build knowledge in that area, find other ways to contribute to the project. Get involved with the project & help answer questions about the project. Be an evangelist for the project & share it with the world every-time you can.

Build Projects That Can Help Others

Most open source projects exist because nothing existed previously to solve someone's problem. For example, Linux Torvalds saw the lack of a free kernel & thus started Linux. Anders Hejlsberg wanted to add a type system to a language that doesn't take away all the things that made JavaScript so popular, thus TypeScript was created.

What you might notice from these examples is that these projects were built initially to solve an individual's problems. They slowly evolved into entities that people make open source projects from!

Perhaps your open source project won't be the next Linux or TypeScript, but you can sure as hell build a project that sustains growth by continuously working on it & providing value to the developer ecosystem you're involved in. Otherwise, your open source project might just die a slow & painless death where you're reminded that you created yet another new repository, had an initial drop of code, and came back to visit it years later on accident.

* * *

Up For Grabs

Majority of open source projects have a concept known as "up for grabs" or "good first issue". These are labels in their issue tracker to let people newer to the project know that there are issues that anyone can take, hence the name. These are great issues to get involved in making a contribution to a project you're interested in.

Once you've made the fix, enhancement, or added the functionality, you're ready to send a pull request.

Sending a Pull Request

A pull request is the heart of majority of open source contributions. A pull request is way for you to tell the project maintainer that they should consider taking in your contribution into the project. This is where code reviews will happen, changes are made, releases are considered, and much more all through a simple request.

If you're interested more in learning about pull requests, do a google search about "GitHub Flow" & you'll learn plenty about it.

Asking & Answering Questions

As a professional problem solver, you have two main tools you can use to solve problems. Those tools are asking & answering questions. These questions can be questions you have about something, questions others might have about something, or really just about any question out there to get a better understanding of how things work.

Stack Overflow

The holy bible for software developers is Stack Overflow. It's a website where you can ask & answer questions about programming topics. Majority of people who use stack overflow don't do anything other than copy & paste from something they find in their favorite search engine, but the real power of understanding comes from asking & answering questions on the site itself.

Think of it this way. If people are copying & pasting your answers, comments, or even your questions, then you are on the other side of understanding. You are following your curiosity far enough to seek an answer to a question or provide somebody else with that knowledge you already possess.

One thing that people don't talk about is how asking questions & answering them on Stack Overflow is actually beneficial to your success as a developer. Being able to show that you have a reputation with examples of how you might help others is a great thing to show to employers. It also can lead to people seeking you out directly based on something you posted on the website.

Your interactions on Stack Overflow can add-up quickly too. For example, I took a few months of maybe 30 minutes a day answering 1-2 questions totaling about ~300 answers. For those 300 answers, I have impacted over 550 thousand people in the world. Although I answered questions years ago, people still occasionally email & send opportunities my way because I invested a little bit of time here & employers find it very impressive that you have a reputation on a platform where most do not.

GitHub

Similar to Stack Overflow, the second largest developer search engine is GitHub in my eyes. GitHub has a longer standing public ledger than Stack Overflow does. People will find your comments, issues, pull requests, and even commits from searching. GitHub is similar to Stack Overflow with regards to asking & answering questions but without the reputation element.

By working in open source, you can start to put your own footprint on the open source map. If you do this enough in your favorite projects, it's very possible that you can start to build a name for yourself as an authority & in certain cases you might even be the first person the project maintainers think about when considering opening a role to work on the project full-time.

So when you come across issues, pull requests, and other artifacts on GitHub where you can help provide clarification, answers, or even questions that everybody is thinking to help improve a project, do it!

These interactions can lead to many opportunities similar to Stack Overflow & just helps you expand your presence as a software developer.

* * *

Twitter

Twitter has often been the software developer's watercooler. There's so many different platforms that serve this purpose, but you can use twitter as a means to provide value regarding the various questions you may have. Since twitter is a bit less formal, it's usually opinions that are being shared. Your mileage may vary with regards to twitter, but it has personally been a great place to interact with some of your favorite people working on cool projects that you're interested in.

Slack, Discord, IRC, & Mailing Lists

Most project teams have a central messaging platform that they use where you can interact in and ask/answer questions about the project or framework. By interacting here, you can be more included in the actual development process & the types of design discussions that are being made in a team setting.

Not all messaging platforms are created equal and there's no standard for what the project will use. Some older projects still use mailing lists & IRC. Some newer projects have moved to newer platforms like slack & discord. Whatever the platform is, you'll want to be included if you're interested in the project & becoming a bigger part of it.

Blogs

Last but not least is your own personal blog or other people's blogs. You can ask and answer any question that is on your mind on your personal blog. You can also ask & help answer questions on other people's blogs if you come across them which in many cases will be largely appreciated by others.

Sometimes it's best to take a problem you have, piece together different perspectives & answers on the problem using all the platforms discussed above and creating a centralized blog that contains an answer. This is a popular way to get search traffic to your personal website & can be helpful to others in the long term.

Blogging Your Progress

By now, you probably know that blogging is one of the most impactful things you can do for your developer career. We're going to talk about how you can structure your blogs in a way that helps you learn & readers will enjoy.

Blogger's Journey

Think of your blog as your individual journey through adversity. You're the main character in which you have something that you want at the end of the day. What is that thing you want? Is it to accomplish something through programming? Is it to put together a sample demonstrating a prototype? Whatever it is, you have something that you want out of writing the blog. Maybe that's even sharing your learnings with the world because you thought it was interesting.

The Blogger's Challenge

What is the primary challenge you're going through and why can't you get what you want today? What are the stakes of this challenge and what will happen if you can't get what you want? Is it high stakes? Is it lower stakes? Does it really matter? All of these questions help you set the stage for the challenge the reader should know about.

The Blogger's Solution

What has now helped you through the challenge? Was it somebody else's blog or answer on a website? Was it a hidden documentation piece that took you hours to find? Whatever it might be, this helps tell the "how" you were eventually able to overcome the challenge.

The Blogger's Transformation

Now is the big take-away moment. How have you been transformed by the experience you went through with regards to identifying a challenge, taking on that challenge, overcoming that challenge, and now you're looking back at it. This can sometimes be the most interesting aspects of a blog. You may have not known anything about the subject today, you learned about it and shared it with the world, but how has that changed you personally?

Formatting Your Journey

If there's any format that you should follow with regards to your blogs, it's this.

* * *

- Start with the challenge or reason you were called to write the blog.
- Talk about the resources, people, or things that helped aide you in understanding the challenge.
- Go over the revelation of the solution you found from all of the help so far.
- Finalize with your learnings from the transformation of the experience as a whole.

Tweeting Your Journey

Twitter can be a great resource to micro-blog your developer journey. I'm going to share some tips that I think will help you grow on twitter without having to become addicted to the platform.

Tell Me Why I Should Follow You

The first thing you should do is update your bio to provide a valuable description as to why I should follow you. You have about 5 seconds to describe to me why I might want to follow a random stranger on the internet. What type of future value will you provide to me as someone who follows your developer journey? What type of development are you doing? What type of projects are you working on? What do you want to become in the future? All those types of things will help me understand why I should follow you.

Building Credibility

You can build credibility simply by providing people value. Value can come from many different ways. What it's mostly about is giving something to the reader something that they find value in. This means that somebody will stop scrolling on Twitter to read your tweet and won't regret reading what you have to say.

You can follow the exact same format in the previous chapter about blogging to build credibility by telling your developer journey through small tweetstorms or threads.

Inspiration of What To Tweet

Reflect at the end of your day as a developer or someone learning to become a developer, what was interesting that happened today? **Tweet** it.

What about the things that took you a lot of effort to figure out? **Tweet it.**

How about the podcasts, youtube videos, or conversations you listen to or had with other people? **Tweet it.**

Making a decision that might be tough such as what technology you're learning next, what company you're going to interview at, or quitting your job to freelance? **Tweet it.**

Found someone else's great work that's a bit outdated and you were inspired to build upon it with new context? **Tweet it.**

Give Give Give Give Then Ask

The world of twitter is more open to people who continue to give than those who ask. The more that you continue to give on twitter, the more credibility you build to the point where when you need to ask for something, people will be more than willing to do so.

Get into the habit of give, give, give, give, and then ask. For every 4 tweets you provide someone value, there is 1 tweet you can ask for someone else's value.

Don't Be A Nuisance, Don't Be Boring

What not to tweet is just as important as what you should tweet. Your authenticity can have a price if it is boring or uninteresting. Remember, you don't have an obligation to share everything on twitter, just the things that other people find value in. So if there's one thing that you can do, that is to find the intersection of what interests you, what interests your potential audience, and what you can build credibility with. Just know that the easiest way to know if you are providing people value is that if what you're posting is not interesting, you will likely be tuned out with lower engagement, or simply unfollowed. When you start to notice these patterns, think back to what can provide value to people.

* * *

Adjust and Adapt

Twitter is not a perfect platform. It's a great platform for sharing small aspects of your developer journey and meeting others on their own journeys. I personally used twitter primarily to consume other people's content, but I can say that if you just dedicate time to producing content for other people to consume, you can see some staggering results in no time if that's your thing. Like everything in software, twitter is simply a tool you can use to create opportunities for yourself.

Project-Based Learning

Side projects are the best way to learn just about anything. Project-based learning is a proven method to learn rapidly as it combines both your natural curiosity of building something you're interested in alongside practical skills to achieve it.

Solve Your Own Problems

Most importantly with project-based learning is that you must solve your own problems or things that you find interesting. Your side projects shouldn't have you dwelling the day you have to work on them. Instead they should excite you every-time you're able to work on them.

One of the best ways to find ideas for your side projects is to scratch an itch of your own. Have a problem in everyday life that you believe can be solved if it was automated? Build it! Always wondered if something would be better if it could do X, Y, or Z? Build it. The possibilities are endless when you solve your own problems, just know that you should limit how many of your own problems you may take on at a time or else it can become unwieldy quickly!

Start Small And Grow Bigger

At most companies and startups you'll hear the concept of "MVP" or minimal viable product. You should consider most of your side projects to be of a MVP quality. This is all fancy speak for saying that your side projects should just be prototypes & as you release them into the world for other people to use, you can grow them with time & effort.

* * *

Create a list of projects and keep track of them

Everyday you might think of a new project you can work on. There's even lists online of people who share their daily ideas for different projects for other people to build. Every time that you have a new idea for a project, you should write it down somewhere. Many great ideas need time to marinate & although you may not pursue it today, it becomes a fun exercise to look back on all the shitty project ideas you've come up with and the nuggets of gold here and there that get you excited to start your next project.

Build fast and minimal

Earlier we talked about creating projects that are scoped to be prototype quality. One main consideration of building fast and minimal is actually in how much time you spend on a side project. Here's a rule that I've followed for years with varying degrees of success. Do not spend more than a month on a side project at a time. This is for various purposes. The first is that we often get extremely excited about our next project to which we start to lose interest in the current project we're working on. We also think about the whole "field of dreams" mentality of if we build it, people will miraculously come use it.

Instead, we should get out of that mindset and put a reasonable time-block of how much time we spend on a specific side project. We can always revisit the side project after a month & pickup where we left off. A month is a great amount of time because it allows us just enough time to get excited, build something of value, and share it with the world.

Don't Obsess Over The Perfect Stack

If there's one thing that tends to be a common occurrence in a developer's side project graveyard, it's an excessive amount of projects that try to perfect the stack of technologies being used to accomplish what the project is about in the first place.

Don't fall into this trap of needing to have the perfect stack before you proceed with the actual idea. Rather, just use what is most familiar or pickup a new language/framework as a basis to learn and make mistakes with. Nothing is ever going to be perfect, so getting in the mindset of "always be coding" is better than nothing.

Build With Constraints

The real world of software is full of constraints and decisions developers had to make in a creative setting. Building side projects with constraints can be a fun way to challenge yourself to do something unique. What if you built a SaaS concept only with vanilla php? How about creating a Diablo 2 clone of the first act in Unity? Whatever the constraint might be, it can help you not overthink the project & focus purely on getting further in the development of the project. Constraints can make it much easier to get to a definition of done so that you can move on to the next project.

Inspiration Tips

Here are a few exercises you can use when it comes down to coming up & working on your next great project idea:

- Schedule It - Put some time down on the calendar to commit yourself to working on your project.
- Add Limitations - Build with constraints to make yourself more productive and focus on finishing.
- Imitate Then Innovate - Copy or mimic a project that inspires you and then innovate on-top of it.
- Use New Techniques / Frameworks - Apply new tech & frameworks towards your project.

Kill Your Darlings

You can't be perfect. In fact, the harder you try to be perfect, the less likely you'll accomplish your goals.

Perfectionism haunts us. We want everything that we ship to be 100% complete. Our internal voices keep telling us things like:

- Are you sure this is good enough?
- Don't you want to code a little more?
- This is going to fail.

Shutting Up Your Mind

We need to shut down the voice in our heads and ship things even if we don't think they're ready.
Good enough is fine enough to ship.

Telling ourselves that just another week or two will improve the deliverable is a lie. Majority of the time people won't even notice. Nobody is going to notice the last 10%, except for us. When people start to take notice, then you can worry about it. But for the sake of your sanity, get in the mindset of shipping early and often, the agile way.

☹Suck at more things

You need to suck at more things on purpose so you're free to be amazing at other things. By strategically choosing which areas you'll accept to be incompetent in, you can prioritize your strengths.

Nobody expects you to be good at everything, so use this as a superpower to better off your strengths. Don't be afraid to not know something, and don't bother learning something that you don't see the initial appeal in even if everyone and their dog is talking about it. It is okay to suck at things.

▒Tips for finishing

There are many things that prevent you from fully finishing. Here's a few things you can do today to cure your perfectionism preventing you from finishing:

- Cut your goal in half today. Ship at 50%.
- Do not let any last-minute doubts prevent you from delivering.
- Track your progress at any time you feel like you haven't moved forward.
- Make it fun.

There are many forces working against you that can block you from doing your best work. We need to identify any type of block and work through them.

Fear

Fear is a common blocking feeling. Do you fear you're not good enough? That you don't know enough? That people will judge what you produce?

Here's the thing. You are going to fail, time after time. The more you fail, the easier it is to overcome fear. You'll fail so often in fact that you will embrace fear as a feeling that you are doing the right things.

Having the fear that you're not good enough, or that you don't know enough is the best type of humility rather than thinking you are the best.

Turn that fear into humility, humility into motivation, motivation into hard work, and hard work into success.

Procrastination

Procrastination has a negative connotation to it, however everyone does it. You will find a way to put off what you're supposed to be doing. You might do that for hours, days, weeks, months, or even years. Procrastination is not something you should eliminate though. Rather you should embrace it as your natural instinct telling you that:

- Your goal isn't clear enough to motivate you.
- You're not having enough fun doing it.
- Your willpower is low for this task.

You can accommodate procrastination by letting it take it's course. For whatever it takes over, you must make up for it the following day. By procrastinating, you are allowing your brain to work through the problem subconsciously.

Distractions

You're going to get distracting by someone or something. Anytime you sit down to work and something intrudes your concentration, it's going to take you anywhere from 15-45 minutes to get back into the flow of work.

Ask yourself how serious you are about reaching your goals. Use Digital Minimalism and set productive habits to avoid any distractions.

▌Homework #8 - Build In Public

By now you should see the value of building in the public, contributing to open source, asking & answering questions, blogging your journey, and even using twitter to share what projects you're working on and why.

Here's what you should do:

- Create a GitHub, Stack Overflow, and Twitter account to get started with documenting your journey. These are just a few to name, but choose the ones you vibe with most.
- Create a blog using a CMS like Wordpress, Ghost, or even build your own blog with a static site generator. Your goal is to publish regular content.
- Write a blog article about your development journey regularly. Start with monthly and work your way towards weekly. Your goal will be 4 blogs over the next 4 months!
- When browsing through answers on question sites or blogs, consider providing comments, answers, or even writing your own blogs about the problem you just solved.

CHAPTER NINE

Career

* * *

Finding growth and new opportunities.

* * *

Finding a Mentor

One of the most impactful things you can do in your career is finding a mentor. Mentors benefit you in more ways than you can imagine. They give you unique perspectives that you may not have seen previously. They can also lead you on the right path earlier and more often when they see you go astray.

Just Ask Someone You Admire

The easiest way to find a mentor is to ask somebody whose work you admire to mentor you. Plain and simple. Ask them out to lunch or if they can spare 30 minutes every other week or month. That 30 minutes can save years on your career advancement by asking the right questions. Don't ask too much of somebody, but also know that asking somebody often is quite a humbling experience & most of the time they will be able to accommodate and help you out.

Informal Mentorship

You can also find mentorship through an informal means. What does this mean exactly? Well this means that you find opportunities in everyday work to learn & seek mentorship from others in casual settings. You might go to lunch with your team & bounce questions off people. You might go out for drinks with a few co-workers to get their perspectives on things around the office. You might even ask somebody for 5 minutes of their time every so-often even though you only know them from the internet.

Where to Find Mentors

Mentors can come from just about everywhere in life. You may contribute to an open source project and find someone who is working on a project that you aspire to be like one day. You may have a co-worker who is really good at something and you want to get just as good as them. You may even meet somebody at a hack-a-thon or tech event & become astonished about how somebody can know so much about tech and business.

Regardless of where you may stumble upon someone's work, follow the simple rule of getting uncomfortable by asking somebody if you can learn from them. If you think about it, the worst that they can say is no. This simple question can lead to some of the best ways to learn about new things very quickly. Having a mentor can be a sounding board of dumb ideas to make them great ideas. A mentor can steer you back to earth when you get sidetracked. Sometimes its as simple as just asking. You'd be surprised at how humbled people would be at the thought.

So look high and look low. Look in open source, look on Twitter, look on TikTok, look on YouTube, look for local meetups, look on LinkedIn, look at developer conferences, look in recently published books or papers, look really anywhere you believe your ideal mentor might be.

🐜 Become the mentor you wish you had
The golden rule of mentorship is that whenever you have an opportunity to mentor somebody, even if it's for the little thing is to be the mentor that you wish you had in the moment. Go the extra mile, be a good resource, and most importantly, be helpful. People are coming to you for help, and you can make it a learning opportunity by being the mentor you wish you had in that very moment.

🤔 Individual Contributor or Manager
Most companies are structured to have two primary discipline tracks with regards to your career. The first is an individual contributor in which you'll be contributing something individually to a company such as code, technical designs, deliverables, specs, support, and much more. The second is a people manager in which you'll be responsible for contributing towards the growth of individual contributors by coaching and leading them towards success.

📸 What you're good at
You'll have a work style that you prefer at a certain point in your career. If you like to work on hard problems, get hands on, and spend majority of your day focused on coding, you're likely going to be an individual contributor.

If you like to work on building teams, solving people problems, and spending the majority of your day in meetings, you're likely going to be a people manager.

* * *

It is really important to know your career trajectory early because it can be your ticket to understanding how to grow in the company you're working at. If you are in a role today that you don't like, you'll want to make a jump to the right track as early as possible. Just know that later on in your career you may want to use your expertise of being an individual contributor to manage them. However know that majority of the time, individual contributors don't want to be managed.

🎸 Too good to manage

When you're really good at your job of being an individual contributor, you are really a "self managed" contributor. What this means is that your manager is really just trying to get out of your way because they know how much value you provide to the company & them micromanaging you can actually cost them in the long run.

Great individual contributors tend to be the people who only go into management when they feel that the job cannot get done unless they do it on other's behalf. This is a great problem to have as those great individual contributors tend to know how to what makes a team happy and productive.

On the other hand, you may have lower performers going into management which can cause even more problems for you down the road. When you notice this becomes the norm at the company you're working at, it may be a sign to think about your career trajectory or even consider working elsewhere.

Companies simply cannot afford their high performers to be promoted, take on excess responsibilities, or even be promoted into management. They need you where you are right now. As you imagine, this is extremely unfair and this sadly is the reality that we live in as developers, but do know that knowing how the game is played can help you discern your future & overall career.

💥Exponential Impact

People management at larger companies tends to bring exponential impact in comparison to an individual contributor. Another sad reality is that people managers tend to be more recognized than individual contributors simply by having headcount underneath them.

People managers who have multiple rockstar performers may demonstrate that they are also a rockstar manager themselves. It's fairly rare that this is the case, but it's not unheard of. Many rockstar individual contributors can see right through this and will often leave bad managers if they feel like they are being held back or not being credited appropriately.

Leadership Potential

Finally, there is a tendency to look for leaders within groups by the leadership teams and middle management groups. If you show leadership potential in a group setting by taking the initiative, making things happen, or being the point person for certain topics, you may have a great opportunity towards being a tech lead or engineering manager in the future. It really just depends on your preference of being an IC vs manager at the end of the day, but do know that you have options if you demonstrate leadership from the ground up and people start to notice it.

I-Shape vs. T-Shape Knowledge

There are different types of knowledge you develop as a programmer. The first is a depth-first knowledge in which you more or less become a specialist in a certain topic or area. The second is a breadth-first knowledge in which you are a generalist in a breadth of topics or areas.

Generalist & Specialist

Early in your career you may be more of a generalist. This is mostly due to exposure and experience that you'll have in the field. One big challenge with being more of a generalist is that you'll be able to do just about any task. As you may imagine that's both a pro and a con. On the opposite end, being a specialist can actually pigeonhole you into certain types of jobs, roles, or even tasks that may get repetitive or boring after a long enough time.

The decision of whether to be more I-shaped or T-shaped with your knowledge really comes down to your interests in the work and things you're learning.

* * *

Niching Down

I was a generalist for the first few years of my career, once I was exposed to mobile development, I quickly turned into the "Android guy" where I was the specialist in the room for anything about developing apps for Android. After a couple more years, I realized I didn't really care that much for Android as although the Android Open Source Project was really cool and interesting, I found myself more interested in other things.

Niching down should become a thing when you're extremely passionate about something. Maybe you're passionate about a specific database technology. Maybe it's a new web standard coming out. Whatever it might be, sometimes opportunity is as simple as niching down to the things you are passionate & curious about.

Become the Subject Matter Expert

When you've niched down on a topic or area, you'll know that you've become the subject matter expert (SME for short) when people come to you for your knowledge or your ability to pickup something extremely quickly. Additionally, opportunities may come your way when people get word that you're the person who has the most experience in a certain topic. Because programming & technology is such a wide array of areas, being the subject matter expert in a particular topic can be quite valuable.

New Opportunities

There will come many opportunities as a developer that you can pursue. Only you will know if they are worthwhile to do so, bt we'll talk a little bit about where they come from and how they might shape your career.

Job Opportunities

First and foremost, job opportunities are a dime a dozen. You'll continuously have recruiters reaching out to you in hopes of joining their startup or company. Not all opportunities are the same in this regard. In fact, majority of job opportunities that come to you from recruiters are ones you may want to actively avoid.

* * *

The good opportunities are ones that come from contributing towards a cause you believe in or a position that you're actively pursing yourself because you believe in the company. Working in the public or finding companies that are doing cool shit are the type of opportunities that I think you should pursue instead.

Project Opportunities

When there are project opportunities that come up and you can become involved, this is something you should jump on earlier than later. Whether it's a new OSS project or exciting new thing at work, these opportunities tend to challenge & reward you in the short term. These short term opportunities can lead to long term opportunities over your career. That OSS project that you contribute to in your free time might end up becoming a full time job with even more opportunities. That new project at work might become the company's next innovative piece of technology. You never really know, but embracing the change is typically a good thing.

Learning Or Earning

Here's a simple rule to follow regarding taking on new opportunities. If you aren't learning or earning in your current opportunity, it may be time to move on. Depending on where you are in life, you may even consider one of these to determine whether or not it's time to move on. For example, you might be earning great money today, but you aren't really learning anything new. If that's something that you truly value in your career, you might make a move to find something you're interested in working on every day. On the other hand, if you aren't earning up to your potential right now but learning a ton everyday, you might reach a threshold where you believe your skills will allow you to earn more. At a certain point in tech, there will usually be money in whatever opportunity you decide to pursue and the question comes down to growth opportunities instead.

Consulting or Freelancing

You may not really care for a stable full-time job and pursue other avenues of making money independently through consulting or freelancing. Whether you want to live the nomad lifestyle of living in different places working on new things every month, or the freedom it brings of picking up the work that you want to do. There's definitely a niche of becoming a freelance developer to make that happen.

💰 Fixed Price Projects

Many freelance jobs are fixed price projects meaning that somebody is willing to pay a specific amount of money to get a job done. That job could be creating a mobile app, building a backend API, fixing a bug in code, or even making an existing app compliant with new terms. Whatever it might be, you can be making anywhere from $1000-3000 on many fixed price projects by building up a portfolio on popular freelance websites like UpWork.

⏳ Hourly Rates

Another type of work you'll do as a freelancer is work on somebody's project with an hourly rate to a specific amount of hours each week/month/quarter/year. These jobs are typically continuous where help is needed over a span of time rather than a one-time thing. This type of work is mostly around maintenance & development towards a large project milestone. Sometimes there are even jobs in which you're hired for a couple hours just to help another developer/entrepreneur solve a bug in their project/code. Your hourly rate will vary, but you can earn quite a bit of money in a short amount of time this way. It's not unheard of to see hourly rates of $80+ for many of these jobs. This rate of course increases as your track record of freelancing grows with you.

🦪Make Money While You Learn

What many people fail to understand about freelancing is that you do not need to be a great developer to get started and make money while learning. This is a bottom-up approach in which you start to take jobs that challenge your development expertise and you learn how to do something to get paid in return. This is great way to incentivize learning without having to dedicate yourself to a 9-5 gig. You can take on smaller jobs at first that help you learn and become more comfortable with various tech / frameworks, and as you grow you can take on more ambitious jobs while getting paid more.

⏱Part-Time & Full Time Contractor

When you have enough knowledge about a specific topic & people are actively providing you with opportunities (such as contracting), you can take on part-time or full-time contracting work. This type of work is usually done at an fixed price for the project, or paid at your specified hourly rate to work inside a company to accomplish something specific. This type of work is interesting because you're acting like a temporary employee for the company, but instead of benefits, you are getting paid in pure cash. Nothing about this work is different than what we talked about earlier besides the potential to work with more people in collaborative settings.

Contractors tend to have subject matter expertise and help lead development efforts in areas that full time employees may not have much experience in. This is usually a temporary thing until a major milestone has been hit, or can even last a number of years until the project is either absorbed officially by the company, or the efforts are killed off depending on the business's needs.

The Truth About Freelancing and Contract Work
I did freelancing & contracting for many startups and individual gigs for a couple years in my development career. This type of work can be stressful & you're largely on the hook for meeting a client's expectations. That isn't for everyone, especially all the anxiety it can bring when it comes to renewing the contract, finding new work, or even filing your taxes.

Freelance developers come in two main categories in my opinion. Inexperienced and over-experienced. Freelance sites are very competitive because there is an excess amount of inexperienced developers from many different locations trying to get experience & paid at the same time. The challenge here is that the quality of the work is drastically low and not much more than what you might find from somebody copying and pasting directly from Stack Overflow.
Over-experienced freelancers on the other hand are quite professional and choose the work they are interested in because they have leverage to do by meeting expectations constantly. You won't have to worry about these people or even them bidding on the jobs you might take on as they tend to always have a queue of work to choose from the highest bidders.

In my opinion, freelancing is one of the main ways you can work as a developer if you prefer the lifestyle. Do know that it can also suck the soul out of you from the amount of hours & stress it can bring. While it may make you grow grey hair faster than you want, it can also grow your bank account in result.

📢Speaking Up

Many people get stuck in a job or position they aren't happy with. The glorious thing about this is that you usually can fix it by talking about it. That's often all that's needed. Simply a conversation. The challenge is that taking the step to speaking up doesn't always mean you know what to say.

♠High Stakes

Think of it this way. The stakes are going to be high if you decide to speak up and if you don't speak up. Especially when it comes down to your happiness and sense of fulfillment, it can often mean to built up resentment when you can be on the track towards your next large goal. Life is too short to not bring up the things that bother you and largely disturb you where you spend majority of your waking time at. You need to be able to build a reputation as someone who can navigate tough situations with grace. The more you speak up appropriately, the more likely you'll improve your career and relationships.

You don't have to be the villain when bringing things up. It's not a game of cat & mouse where you're the adversary. There's not going to be a magic wand for every situation you encounter, but having a conversation is a good start. Most people are reasonable and will want to know if there's something you're unhappy about. You don't have to be a jerk to reasonable people. You can do it gracefully and collaboratively even when the stakes are high.

🤖Your Boss Is Human

If you put your boss on a pedestal, you will have already defined the power dynamic between the two of you. The opposite is also true, if your boss treats you like someone underneath them, you may have an unfortunate power dynamic going on.

Here's the trick to it all, you will always get best results when you approach your boss as if they are a normal human. Not royalty or someone who is out to get you, but rather a normal ass human-being.

Don't overthink how you talk to them. You don't need to calculate every move and have another job lined up just to talk, but rather just be direct and straightforward. As humans, sometimes our emotions can get in the way. It doesn't mean that you can't have emotions, but rather you can't let them take over the conversation.

Detach Your Relationship

One of the most effective ways to speak up is to detach your relationship when talking to somebody like your boss or a coworker. Although you should always keep the relationship as close as possible when talking like humans, think of you speaking up as a means to what would benefit the group, organization, or company most. This way you can take an approach as to what's in the best interests of all rather than just yourself.

Temporary to permanent change

If there's a hesitation to making drastic change in your career such as working from home, how meetings are conducted, the projects you're working on, etc you should consider asking for a short-term experiment that helps lower the stakes and gives you the opportunity to demonstrate first hand the effectiveness. One thing I would do in my career was that I would tell my employer that I want to work from home full-time. When I expressed this concern, my employer would give me a couple days a week to try it out. After a few months of this experiment, I convinced my bosses to let me work from home permanently. They saw the benefit of this, and I've been doing it for the entirety of my career.

The Job You Signed Up For

Let's face it, the more experience you get at a company, the more responsibilities you will take on and inherit. This however can be a double-edged sword as it can severely impact your actual effectiveness in the workplace. Maybe there was that one time where you took on something because nobody else would and you're stuck doing it. These should be talked about because they are a daily burden to our work. You can't juggle everything even in the most senior roles at a company. Every job has it's own limits, and you should be setting boundaries for the type of work that you're interested in, and the type of work that you are not so interested in.

Taking On More Responsibility

When you start to feel confident that you've proved yourself in your current role and want to extend it, you should be asking about taking on more responsibility. You have to be specific with this however. Do you want to take on bigger projects? Do you want to lead people? Do you want to help the company in another way? Whatever it might be, you should think through the details and talk about them.

Homework #9 - Job or Career?

By now you should have a good idea of how to find a mentor, what type of career tracks there are, the types of knowledge, when to take new opportunities, doing consulting work, and speaking up when you don't feel heard.

Here's what you should do:

- Find at least one mentor this year even if that's a 30 minute conversation over coffee once. The more the merrier as you can learn everyone. All you have to do is ask.
- Make a 5 year career plan and set thresholds for where you want to be in 1 years time, 2 years time, and 5 years time. This should include how often you are promoted, what type of contracts you might take on (if consulting), and what you want to be working on.
- Do research on the current freelance market and the technologies you're learning or proficient in. Consider taking on a few contracts for some extra experience.
- If you're in a job you don't like right now and you haven't spoke up to raise your concerns, consider doing it while looking for new opportunities.

CHAPTER TEN

Validate

* * *

VALIDATE

✓

Come up with ideas that stick.

* * *

How To Come Up With Ideas

Although side projects are one way to see your ideas through, you may want to validate ideas with the public to understand if there's a potential opportunity to monetize your time and effort to find what's known as "product market fit". This is when you know people will willingly pay for your product as it provides them some type of value.

Have Unique Experiences

One of the best ways to come up with ideas regarding problems that people may have is to live a unique life. Have fun experiences, live life to the fullest and you'll start to have ideas that represent crazy concepts that others may see value from.

Start With Your Problems

Your everyday problems are the best thing to start from. Not only do you understand the problem more intimately than others would, but you've also experienced it first hand. The common thinking around solving your own problems is that other people in the world are bound to have the same problem as you some point in their lives.

Niche Down

Sometimes solving generic problems can be too difficult or even too broad. Instead, you may want to niche down into something more specific. Your problem might not be a problem for every person in the world, but rather it might be a problem for a certain type of hobbyists like yourself. That's what it means by niching down. It's scoping the problem towards a specific demographic of people who are willing to pay you money to solve it.

How To Make A Million Dollars

The reason you may niche down is that you can charge more money to specific groups of people. For example, if you built a software product for rich doctors or lawyers, you might be able to charge more as you may be saving them a significant amount of money compared to the average person.

Here's how you might make a million dollars with software depending on if you niche or not.

- $5000 product for 200 people
- $2000 product for 500 people
- $1000 product for 1000 people
- $200 product for 5000 people
- $100 product for 10000 people
- $10 product for 100000 people

- 500 people pay $167/month for 1 year
- 1000 people pay $83/month for 1 year
- 2000 people pay $42/month for 1 year
- 5000 people pay $17/month for 1 year
- 10000 people pay $9/month for 1 year

🩺Micro Niche

Now that you understand the power of niching, you might also want to consider micro-niching or even niching down further. A rich doctor or lawyer might be a specific type of doctor or lawyer. These specific niches help you get higher up on the funnel to a specialization. For example, if you built an app for dermatologists, you might be able to sell this to various dermatology groups. However if you built an app for cosmetic dermatologists, you would be micro niching to even more specific needs.

🩹 Micro To Multi Niche

Now that you might have found a micro niche, you might be able to expand your idea into multiple micro niches. Perhaps that app for cosmetic dermatologists can also be sold to pediatric dermatologists and Mohs surgeons. Now you've gone multi niche.

👨‍⚕️ Multi Niche to Adjacent Markets

Say that you have success with multi niches and you are finding similarities with other specializations. Now you can sell your app to other specialists such as audiologists, optometrists, and dentists. You've just entered the adjacent markets.

* * *

Adjacent Markets to Platform

Last but not least, you may have struck gold to the point where your app can be made into a platform for various healthcare specialists to use everyday. You've now become a big successful entity by starting as small as possible. So while you can think big with regards to your ideas, you're better off thinking small first and growing overtime!

Think Boring, Not Mind-blowing

Your ideas do not have to be mind-blowing for them to be useful. Ideas tend to be a dime a dozen, but great execution will separate it from the rest. People want convenience, reliability, and value. If your idea is boring and serves many of these purposes, people will also have no problem handing you their hard earned cash.

Good Ideas Usually Stick

The best ideas usually stick around. They have something about them that keep us thinking. Whether that's the convenience of connecting with a random stranger you just met in person, the ability to hail a personal driver anywhere you are, or being able to buy a book directly on the internet. If you think about it, these concepts are nothing new. They are actually old ideas adopted to the new world we live in. They each provide us some type of convenience, reliability, and ultimate value at the end of the day.

Painpoint Framework

When working closely with your potential customers, you can use what's known as a painpoint framework to help you get the critical feedback to validate and make your product better. This framework is based on my personal framework that I use at Microsoft to help build products scaling hundreds of thousands of users. A painpoint framework helps you build empathy with your users while being able to validate real solutions that will make your future customers happier & your pockets deeper.

Painpoint Questions

There are 6 simple questions you can ask somebody regarding the problem you're trying to solve and whether or not your solution is valuable to them. These questions are:

* * *

- What is your most consistent and present problem today?
- How are you going about solving this problem right now?
- What happens if you don't solve this problem?
- How painful is this problem for you on a scale 1-10?
- If you could wave a magic wand to solve this problem, how would you solve it?
- Would that solution be worth paying for? If so, how much?

Now let's dive into each of these questions a bit further to help you understand why they are useful.

What is your most consistent and present problem today?

When building a product to solve somebody's pain, we need to ensure that the problem is actually on the top of mind for the person. If we find that our software / app does not solve a problem that is regularly brought up by individuals when asking this question, we may be working on something that doesn't provide value to our potential users.

How are you going about solving this problem right now?

Your product likely solves a problem that people have today and makes it easier, automates it, or provides some type of value to assist in solving a problem. When we learn from our users how they are currently approaching the problem, we get ideas for how we can expand our product or even add new functionality for workflows we were never aware of in the first place.

What happens if you don't solve this problem?

What if there is no solution to the problem? This will typically make the users feel a specific way such as frustrated, sad, or even disappointed. By tapping into the emotions of your potential users, you can build some empathy as to the type of emotions you are providing them. Perhaps that might be uplifting them everyday when using your product because they now can automate something they usually wasted 30 minutes in the morning doing.

😖 How painful is this problem for you on a scale of 1 to 10?

How much pain does this problem bring somebody today even if there are potential solutions out in the world? This helps us understand the current stakes of the problem space. If the pain is anywhere from 7+, you will know that you're on the path towards solving something people will find valuable to lessen that pain.

✏ If you could wave a magic wand to solve this problem, how would you solve it?

Now is the fun question that has really no limitations. If they could magically solve the problem, how would they solve it? Listen very closely here because your users will be telling you exactly what your software needs to do in order to provide them enough value that's worth giving you money. Many people may answer this question with completely unrealistic solutions or "it just does" types of answers, but you will often get people who think within the constraints of reality and give you the right results which are absolute gold and will save you both time & money in the future.

💰 Would that solution be worth paying for? If so, how much?

Finally, the question that validates everything before it and probably the motivation behind building something new in the first place. By asking people if the solution they thought up of or the solution you may have shown them already is worth paying for, you'll be able to get a grasp for how much somebody values the problem being solved. Asking them how much they'd be willing to pay gives you an idea of how much you can charge your customers given how they value the resolution to their current pain.

!? Keep these questions in the back of your head

These questions are some of the most valuable questions I have asked individuals in my career. Each of these questions can be used at different stages of validating your product, but when used together you can get a holistic understanding of the value you will be providing to someone else. Keep these questions in the back of your head so you can use them when you need to. Most of the time a 30-minute call or survey is the best medium to use these questions. I've personally found the magic wand question to provoke the most interesting thoughts when it comes to validating a product.

* * *

Talking To Users

Engaging with your users is the only way to be in touch with their needs. Not connecting with your users can lead to disconnected & unhappy people. Although it may make us feel uncomfortable at first to talk to our users, it's crucial to being successful in meeting their needs.

ABC's of Product Development

The ABCs of product development can be simplified in statements like "Always Be Connecting" &
"Always Be Coding". Following the idea of being Agile, we want to consistently provide value to users by connecting & developing features, fixing bugs, and planning future work to meet their needs.

How To Talk To People

There's really nothing complicated as to how you connect with the people who may use your product at the end of the day. There's so many mediums in which you might talk to people at the end of the day on like Facebook, Twitter, Reddit, Product Hunt, YouTube, TikTok, and many many more. The most important thing is that you are actively talking to people and using the painpoint framework we talked about earlier to truly understand their needs.

30-Minute Interviews or Private Chats

You can accomplish much more in a 30-minute interview with a potential user than you might over many different messages back and forth on a public forum. Although these public forums can be useful for capturing general feedback, many people are quite reserved when they are interacting in the public as opposed to talking to you in private. If you can take the conversation to a more private means between you and another person, the higher fidelity of feedback you'll receive.

Feedback Loops

Keeping your feedback loops between your users & the development of your software as short as possible will help you stay connected towards your validation journey of landing your first paid customers. By continuing to keep users involved in the development & sending them updates that include the progression of the development is key.

Minimum Viable Product

Your MVP or minimum viable product is the smallest working prototype that test your hypothesis against real people to learn about your product fitting in the market you're trying to sell it in.

Testing Hypotheses

The point of a MVP is to collect as much possible learning about your customers with the least amount of effort. You can think of this as building enough of a product to be valuable & useful which will help set the tone for how much value your potential users receive from it. This helps us take our hypotheses about what we think we know about the problems, the market, and our solution and puts them to the test with real people.

Does One Thing Well

Since MVPs are more prototype-like than a full product, they should focus on doing one thing well. Including too many features or covering too many use-cases can be detrimental to understanding if the product is viable to the people we think it is viable for. This helps us reduce the amount of time we will spend engineering the product, but also get it in the hands of customers as soon as possible to ensure that one thing it does well solves the needs for customers to be willing to pay for it.

Easy To Provide Feedback

Because the focus of an MVP is collecting feedback, it is extremely important that users have ample means to provide you feedback. Whether that is unique ways to do that within the product by allowing users to message and email you directly, or even collecting rich telemetry data in the product to understand how users are using the product, this information can help you understand what needs to be further built, improved, or even removed entirely.

* * *

Version 1.0

Your first version of a product is usually considered your MVP. It is when you as an software developer release your product into the market to truly validate your assumptions behind your product or business idea. This tests a combination of your business model, product, and users to see how the market reacts to your first version.

Sharing Your Ideas

Your ideas can be quite unique, but also probably thought of before in somebody else's life at some point. Hiding your ideas from the world prevents them from actually growing, becoming stronger, more resilient, and well...brilliant! Although you may think you have an idea for the next Facebook, Uber, Coinbase, you name it, you probably do, but what ultimately matters is execution on those ideas.

Don't Be Afraid To Share

Ideas are dime a dozen. Everybody has them and there are definitely more bad ideas than good ones out in the world. Your ideas are no different. This is not to insult you in a book that you paid for, but the reality is that many of our ideas are quite bad when they first are thought of. It takes time to digest bad ideas to make them somewhat good ideas, and even more to make them great ideas.

As you may imagine, the great ideas we have are not actually about the idea or thought itself, but rather it's because we've thought through how we may execute upon the idea, and that's what really matters.

Execution Is What Matters

There are hundreds if not thousands of companies that build products around the same ideas, the only thing that separates them is their execution on those ideas. Some companies you may have never heard of take a great idea and poorly execute on it to which they no longer are a company. Some companies you may have heard of take a great idea and have great execution. These companies as you may imagine all started from the same ideas, but execution is what differs them.

* * *

Idea x Execution = Business

- Bad idea = 0
- Good idea = 10
- Great idea = 20
- No execution = $0
- Good execution = $100,000
- Great execution = $1,000,000

Product Market Fit

When your product is meeting the needs of your target customer, you have product market fit. In other words, if someone is willing to pay you money for your product because it does something of value for them, you have product market fit.

When People Sell For You

Think about the last product where you recommended it to everyone you thought would be interested in buying it and they eventually did. That's product market fit. It's when your product fits an unmet need that the value you provide is enough for somebody to tell others about it and can't stop talking about it.

You Can Feel It

You don't need to raise VC capital or have your product go viral to know that you have product market fit. It can be as simple as seeing a regular amount of new users buying or using your product as fast as you can actually make it. In other words, your product is growing faster than you can actually keep up with.

It can be transient

Like everything in the world, product market fit can come and go. One day your app is the hottest thing since sliced bread, and then the following month you're begging people to use it. This is normal. Not every product released to the market will withstand the changing needs of everyday people, but it's not impossible. If you niched down enough to be a product that provides value to users who now rely on it, you may be more resilient to change.

Customer Development

Over the last few chapters, you've learned about how to validate painpoints, customers, and sharing your ideas. This process of validating with your customers is known as customer development. Customer development never really stops once you begin. In fact, customer development never stops while you still have some type of active customers. Being in touch with your customers is the most important thing you can do for sustaining your product relationship with them.

Customer Discovery

By now you probably realize that there's a constant process to determine who your customers are and whether the problem you're solving is valuable to them. Sometimes the customers you identified might be the wrong people, or sometimes your problem is solving the wrong problem.

Discovering your customers is the important thing. Finding the group of people allows you to ask them the right questions through surveys, interviews, and much more.

Customer Validation

As you continue to discover your customers and validate solutions against them, you are building a repeatable sales process in which you are selling the product or even the idea of the product to early customers, which in turn is validating your concept for a business. These early customers become advocates of your product and help your business grow in turn.

Customer Creation

As your business starts to grow, you are creating demand for new customers to use your product. You can widen your funnels as to how you may reach those customers, but overall you have a solid foundation as to being able to create a customer from thin air. In other words, a customer can find you on the internet or hear about your product and purchase it at the same time to which they may become advocates of the product.

Company Building

Last but not least, this whole process helps you create a company that can sustain itself through the product offerings, the cost it takes to keep the product running, how much it may take to acquire new customers, and as you combine these things you may realize that you now have a fully fledged company on your hands that you've built, all by starting with an idea, niching down, building a MVP, and finding product market fit in the process.

Homework #10 - Validate Your Idea

By now you should be able to validate a product idea by asking real people about their painpoints in daily life and getting an understanding for a minimum viable product that they will pay you for.

Here's what you should do:

- Brainstorm problems in your life and the various painpoints around them.
- Go talk to users who likely have the same problems to validate your potential solution against. Use interviews, surveys, and quick-pulses to do this.
- Build up a backlog of feature ideas based on talking to users to your initial minimum viable product.
- Try to build the product MVP and launch it publicly!

CHAPTER ELEVEN
Workflows
* * *

WORKFLOWS

Distraction free deep work.

* * *

👷 Deep & Shallow Work

To find your focus, you need to have a long enough uninterrupted work session to get into the flow state so you can do some of your best work. You can regularly get into the habit of this magical flow state by introducing deep work and shallow work into your regular routine.

💪 Deep Work

You should plan to have at least two deep work sessions every single day. Each of these sessions should last anywhere from 1-4 hours and provide you enough time to enter the flow state while also having enough time to get something significant done. Starting out with an hour and building up the tolerance to longer deep work sessions is ideal.

These deep work sessions serve as a means to have uninterrupted time to work on stuff. At first, these sessions will be hard to get through without feeling bored or distracted. It takes time to build up enough tolerance to work in a focused setting for hours at a time. After you've accomplished your deep work sessions for the day, you should enter the concept of shallow work.

🥄 Shallow Work

Working too long in a focused state of mind isn't sustainable on a day to day basis. Being able to regularly go into a relaxed state of mind after your deep work sessions can help you be more effective for the next day to come.

Shallow work is another name for unfocused or relaxed type of work. This is where you let your brain unconsciously solve problems for you. Whether you choose to give your attention to a television or book is really up to you. Perhaps it's even video games or sports.

The point of shallow work is to get your mind completely off of what you were working on previously in your deep work sessions. This helps your brain come up with more creative solutions and do majority of the work for you so that when you enter your next deep work session, you simply need to show up.

* * *

Daily Routine

Everyday is an opportunity to have two deep work sessions and a long shallow work session. Although your routine will vary depending on how you prefer to live your life, you should prioritize these three time-blocks in your daily routine as much as possible. Consider a typical work day that might run from 9-5pm. You have 8 hours in other words to accomplish something. But wait, you lose at least 1 hour to take a lunch and may get distracted in the morning and afternoon leaving you with maybe a few hours of actual work.

In other words, even if you had only 8 hours to get something done during the day, you have another 8 hours after the fact. You don't have to make the most out of each minute everyday and be some type of productivity guru, but rather you can strive to take those 16 hours and find reasonable time-blocks for your three sessions. Here's an example of my morning routine:

- Wake Up
- Deep Work Session #1
- Lunch
- Deep Work Session #2
- Dinner
- Shallow Work Session
- Sleep

Digital Minimalism

Do you want to be able to exercise regularly, read three to four books a month, and even learn to play an instrument? What about having a closer relationship to your wife and kids? How about succeeding in the workplace and increasing your focus to achieve more?

Although these results do not come easily, you will be much further along your way if you took charge of your digital well-being.

* * *

Digital Well-Being

Many of our digital habits are detrimental to our goals and limited hours in a day. On average, you may use Facebook for up to an hour a day. On-top of this, you may check your phone over 40 times daily. Just think about how much time is being used here alone.

There is nothing wrong with using Facebook, or owning a smart phone. There is however something wrong with mindlessly scrolling through infinite socials feeds in search of validation and a sense of belonging.

By being mindful of our digital well-being, we are being intentional with the technology and setting rules to which we can use it with. I'll go over a few reasons why we should do this below:

Digital Clutter is Taxing – Having an excess amount of devices, applications, services, etc provide many ways to avoid boredom. Having the ability to use these items on virtually any device makes it even more accessible to get stuck in a feedback loop from hell.

Digital Optimization is Important – Being able to figure out what devices, applications, services, etc that bring you the absolute most joy in your life is a must. Secondly, having an intent for each of your devices, applications, and services helps you become more optimal with your limited time each day.

Digital Balance is Freeing – You don't need to feel obligated to take apart of other people's feedback loops. You are focusing on yourself and your close friends and family. You are being more intentional with making those relationships closer as they bring you more joy than being connected online.

* * *

Enter JOMO

JOMO, or what it stands for; Joy of Missing Out is the counterpart to FOMO, or what it stands for; Fear of Missing Out. When interacting with others on social media, texting, or even upcoming technologies, we get a sense of FOMO which prevents us from ever leaving the platforms. We fear that without sending a like or comment to our friend's feeds, they will forget about us. They might forget to invite us to the next happening thing, or they might forget we even exist.

Here's the thing about FOMO. The people who want to be connected with you will go out of their way to ensure that happens. Or vice versa, as you will ensure your relationship exists outside of a social platform.

I like to think of this rather as JOMO, as I don't have to prescribe to other's social feed validation in fear of being missed or forgotten, instead that actually brings me joy because it means I can focus my time and energy on other things.

Being Okay with Alone Time

Having alone time is needed for original and creative thought. Being deprived of it can actually make you deprived of these thoughts. Use alone time as a way to recharge, and know that it's okay and needed to have alone time.

Benefits of Unplugging

Your brain is working quite hard to keep up with all of life's daily distractions alongside all of the digital distractions as well. By unplugging even for a small amount of time every day, you are allowing your brain to focus on your subconscious mind more. This allows for even more original and creative thought. Having a clear mind can help you think and solve hard problems as well.

⚖Tips for Balancing your Digital Life

Below are a number of tips that can help you on your journey to digital well-being:

* * *

• For every device, application, and service, ask yourself if you really need it or use it today. It must bring you absolute joy before you let it into your daily life.

• For each device, application, and service you use, you must give it rules that you abide by to ensure you are not constantly sinking time into them. i.e. Twitter for 10 minutes a day at Noon.

• Use each device with a specific intent such as a cell phone only for communicating with others in personable ways such as texting and calling, or using a computer for programming. Get rid of applications and services on these machines that do not relate with the intent of the device.

• Balance your passive consumption such as watching shows, playing video games, reading books, etc with demanding activities such as going to dinner with a friend, playing board games with family, etc.

• Prioritize demanding activities over passive consumption.

• Find a daily way to disconnect from technology. Go on a long walk, go to the gym, go to a coffee shop, go on a hike, etc all without bringing technology with you. If you do bring technology with you, make sure it follows a specific intention (Emergency contact, Music to listen to, etc)

🧘Distraction Free Work

You can't do your best work if you are in a constant state of distraction. The smart phone on your desk, the web browser watching Twitch, or even friends or family being loud around you. To do your best work, you need to become disciplined towards the types of things that can distract you.

▦ Turn Off The Devices

Being one of the easiest ways to free yourself of distractions, you can simply turn off the devices that are likely going to distract you. Trust me, the text or scrolling endlessly on twitter can wait until you're done and you'll be happy you did it sooner. If you aren't going to use the device, turn it off or put it in another room.

* * *

✋ Block Apps & Websites

If you cannot live without your devices being on near you, then you should go nuclear and limit the access to certain apps and websites on them. For example for every app you might find distracting, you should uninstall it from your phone and re-install it when you want to use it (it's a huge pain, but it works). For websites you constantly use as a distraction, download a website blocker online and start adding them to a list where you can turn them on or off on a schedule or whenever you really need to focus.

🎧 Specific Devices For Specific Work

This next one is a bit hard depending on how many devices you own. If you own one device, then skip over this, but if you own many smart devices such as phones, computers, tablets, and more you should really listen for a second. Instead of using each of these devices as a general all-purpose device to access all your stuff on with just a different form factor consider giving each device a specific job to be done.

For example, your laptop might only be used for coding & writing. Your smartphone might only be used for social media & communicating with other people. Your tablet might only be used for drawing or reading. You may not think this helps at first as it makes the things you regularly do harder, but trust me on this one, this really saves you a ton of time and keeps you focused.

📍 Context Matters

Similar to having similar devices for specific work, you will want to establish some type of context in which you associate an activity with. For example you might associate your bedroom with resting or relaxing and therefore you can do things that don't require much focus in there.

You might go to the local library to really get into the zone for anything that requires focus such as studying or working on a project.

You can even associate objects with the respective context as well. For example, turning on a lamp on your desk might represent how you know you're going to start a deep work session. Opening up your door might represent how you know you're relaxing for the rest of the night. Whatever that may be, try to associate them similarly with activities.

Developing Willpower

Willpower is our ability to restrain impulses to do something. Like muscles in our body, it must be trained. The more willpower you develop, the faster you'll be able to build it. Somewhat of a catch-22, but you'll get what I'm saying later.

When working to develop our willpower, we need to set clear goals for what we want to accomplish and start small to eventually build up.

Willpower comes in three different forms:

- I won't
- I will
- I want

I won't

The type of willpower that you're very familiar of. The ability to say "I won't eat that desert because I'm on a diet" or "I won't play video games when I should be studying for a final".

I will

The type of willpower that will help you do the uncomfortable to get a step closer to your goals. "I will make better habits for my future".

I want

The type of willpower that defines a strong reason and clear why to your goals in life. "I want to become the next CTO at this company".

Our natural instinct

You'll have times in your life where a natural instinct will kick in. Whether it's right after a major life event like getting married or having a kid, or getting older and realizing you aren't where you wanted to be by this time in your life.

* * *

You'll say to yourself "I won't, I will, or I want" at this time and you'll work on your willpower to develop routine to turn your wants into reality.

However, willpower isn't an infinite resource. Everyday we use our willpower and eventually by the end of the day we deplete our willpower supply. However, we can improve our willpower.

Increasing your willpower

Your brain is responsible for your willpower, and taking care of your brain is your top priority. You can improve your willpower for each day by:

- Eating healthy foods
- Meditating for 10 minutes a day
- Exercising regularly
- Sleeping well

Now you may say, Jon, these are things that require willpower in the first place to do consistently. And yes you are right. each of these items require willpower from you to develop more willpower.
Eating unhealthy foods, never working out, and getting less than 8 hours of sleep is going to limit your willpower everyday.

Knowing when you're done

Having awareness of when our willpower is depleted for the day can be very beneficial to us. Letting our minds wander can actually allow our subconscious to kick in and solve complex problems, bring creative ideas, and help us make better decisions overall. Have you ever worked on a complex problem at work and upon banging your head on your desk, you go home and come up with the solution in the shower? That's mindlessness.

Practicing mindlessness is as simple as distracting your mind with something else. Find something that brings you joy to be mindless with.

* * *

What Makes A Good Workflow

Everyone has their own unique way of working. Building your own workflow can take years to perfect & understand what works best for you. There are things that make a workflow great, and there are things that can hinder your workflow. I can only speak on behalf of what I believe makes a good workflow and the common things I try to avoid.

Consistent & Deterministic

A great workflow is consistent and deterministic. What this means is that you are regularly able to complete the workflow with predictable results. Workflows that are not consistent or unpredictable are likely to break flow and have you distracted towards something else. In other words, the more boring and stable you can make your workflow, the better.

One Thing At A Time

Humans are not born to multi-task. You might disagree with that statement but it's largely true. Being able to work on only one thing at a time will benefit you much more in the long run. Do not try to take on too many things in your workflow and only move on to the next thing when you completed the one thing you were hoping to do.

Regular Breaks

You may slice your time in many different ways, but whatever way you decide to do it, make sure you're taking regular breaks. The pomodoro technique for example takes a 5 minute break after 25 minutes of focused work. This means you should likely take a 15 minute break every 90 minutes of focused work.

⚲ Daily Highlight

Aim to have one daily highlight in which if you completed it, it would make your day. This should be a task that you can complete in your workflow that isn't too easy and isn't too hard, but just right. Make it a goal to have one daily highlight that you complete in your workflows.

▓ Homework #11 - Crafting A Workflow

By now you can build a workflow that helps you be productive and get stuff done with deep work, digital minimalism, and distraction free work.

Here's what you should do:

- Build a workflow starting with the total amount of hours you can spend on deep & shallow work.
- Find ways to minimize your digital addiction by blocking websites, apps, and games while you're in a deep work session.
- Craft a ritual where doing a specific context such as putting on noise-cancelling headphones or turning on a desk lamp represents the entering of a deep work session.
- End the deep work session with another context queue as to a natural ending such as turning off a computer or turning on a device for fun.
- Keep an eye on your willpower throughout each day and work on good habits that will build your willpower up overtime like exercise and sleep.

Summary

The Beginning Of Your Journey

You've learned a lot over the course of this book.

- You learned to get into the programmer's mindset.
- You developed a learning system.
- You crafted your own developer roadmap.
- You built the lasting habits.
- You can quickly acquire new skills.
- You realized how to land a job.
- You see the power of the internet by building.
- You know your options with a career.
- You can make products people will pay for with validation.
- And you can create your own productive workflow to get shit done.

While this may be the end of this book, it's just the beginning of your journey. Whether you're new to programming, trying to find your next opportunity, or even wanting to build your own sustainable lifestyle, I hope that this book has inspired you to take your goals to the next level & I wish you the best of luck. See you around the internet friend!

Jon

Books Are Made Of Books

📖 Books Are Made Of Books

- Bird by Bird by Anne Lamontt
- Deep Work by Cal Newport
- Atomic Habits by James Clear
- Hyperfocus by Chris Bailey
- The Practice by Seth Godin
- Anything You Want by Derrick Sivers
- A Mind for Numbers by Barbara Oakley
- Effortless by Greg McKeown
- Algorithms to Live By by Brian Christian and Tom Griffiths
- Tiny Habits by B.J. Fogg
- High Output Management by Andy Grove
- Surely You're Joking Mr. Feynman by Richard Feynman
- The War of Art by Steven Pressfield
- Make It Stick by Peter C. Brown
- Thinking In Systems by Donella H. Meadows
- The Gifts of Imperfection by Brene Brown
- How To Take Smart Notes by Sonke Ahrens
- Make Time by Jake Knapp
- Storyworthy by Matthew Dicks
- Can't Hurt Me by David Goggins
- Range by David Epstein
- Think Like A Rocket Scientist by Ozan Varol
- The Art of Impossible by Steven Kotler
- Creativity by John Cleese
- Working In Public by Nadia Eghbal
- The Art of Doing Science and Engineering by Richard

Made in the USA
Middletown, DE
23 March 2022

63088785R00106